GIVING BACK

GIVING BACK

Using Your Influence to Create Social Change

Merrill J. Oster and Mike Hamel

NAVPRESS

Bringing Truth to Life

P.O. Box 35001, Colorado Springs, Colorado 80935

OUR GUARANTEE TO YOU

We believe so strongly in the message of our books that we are making this quality guarantee to you. If for any reason you are disappointed with the content of this book, return the title page to us with your name and address and we will refund to you the list price of the book. To help us serve you better, please briefly describe why you were disappointed. Mail your refund request to: NavPress, P.O. Box 35002, Colorado Springs, CO 80935.

The Navigators is an international Christian organization. Our mission is to reach, disciple, and equip people to know Christ and to make Him known through successive generations. We envision multitudes of diverse people in the United States and every other nation who have a passionate love for Christ, live a lifestyle of sharing Christ's love, and multiply spiritual laborers among those without Christ.

NavPress is the publishing ministry of The Navigators. NavPress publications help believers learn biblical truth and apply what they learn to their lives and ministries. Our mission is to stimulate spiritual formation among our readers.

www.navpress.com

ISBN 1-57683-386-0 (paperback); ISBN 1-57683-467-0 (hardback)

Cover design by Erik Simmons/The Envoy Group
Interior design by Dana Sherrer/The Envoy Group
Creative Team: Kent Wilson, Greg Clouse, The Envoy Group

Unless otherwise identified, all Scripture quotations in this publication are taken from the HOLY BIBLE: NEW INTERNATIONAL VERSION® (NIV®). Copyright © 1973, 1978, 1984 by International Bible Society. Used by permission of Zondervan Publishing House. All rights reserved. Other versions used include: THE MESSAGE (MSG). Copyright © 1993, 1994, 1995, 1996, 2000, 2001, 2002. Used by permission of NavPress Publishing Group; The Living Bible (TLB), Copyright © 1971, used by permission of Tyndale House Publishers, Inc., Wheaton, IL 60189, all rights reserved.

Library of Congress Cataloging-in-Publication Data
Oster, Merrill J., 1940-
      Giving back : using your influence to create social change / Merrill J. Oster and Mike Hamel.
      p. cm.
Includes bibliographical references.
      ISBN 1-57683-386-0 (pbk.); ISBN 1-57683-467-0 (cloth)
      1. Social action--United States--Case studies. 2. Community organization--United States--Case studies. 3. Voluntarism--United States--Case studies. 4. Church and social problems--United States--Case studies. 5. Social responsibility of business--United States--Case studies. I. Hamel, Mike. II. Title.
      HN65 .O87 2003
      361.2'0973--dc21

                                                                                                2002151985

Printed in the United States of America
1 2 3 4 5 6 7 8 9 10 / 07 06 05 04 03

FOR A FREE CATALOG OF
NAVPRESS BOOKS & BIBLE STUDIES,
CALL 1-800-366-7788 (USA)
OR 1-416-499-4615 (CANADA)

Dedication

*To the men and women of Pinnacle Forum who,
by stewarding this influence, are becoming salt and light
to America's cultural gatekeepers.*

Merrill J. Oster

*To Bruce McNicol and his culture-changing
vision for Leadership Catalyst.*

Mike Hamel

Contents

Preface 9

Introduction **Rules of Engagement** .13
Bob Buford and the age of social entrepreneurs

Chapter One **Follow the (Servant) Leader** 25
Ken Blanchard and The Center For *Faith*Walk Leadership

Chapter Two **Capital Idea: Getting the Most for Your Money** . .35
Juan Benitez and Enterprise Development International

Chapter Three **Beauty from Ashes:**
A Model for Racial Reconciliation 45
Glen Kehrein and Circle Urban Ministries; Abraham Lincoln
Washington and Rock of Our Salvation Church

Chapter Four **A Girl's Best Friend** .57
Elayne Bennett and Best Friends Foundation

Chapter Five **Million Dollar Dream: Profits for Philanthropy** . .69
David Burdine and Bethesda Associates

Chapter Six **Set Free, Stay Free: Prison Reform That Works** . .81
Jerry Wilger and Prison Fellowship's InnerChange Freedom Initiative

Chapter Seven **Investing in Generation Next** 93
Duncan Campbell and Friends of the Children

Chapter Eight **Exporting Hope, One House at a Time** 105
Sean Lambert and Homes of Hope

Chapter Nine **The Power of a Mother's Love** 115
Kit Danley and Neighborhood Ministries

Chapter Ten **How "High" Should Higher Learning Go?** 125
Larry Donnithorne and Colorado Christian University

Chapter Eleven **TreeHouse Outreach:**
                    Offering Hope to Troubled Teens 137
Fred Peterson and Family Hope Services

Chapter Twelve **Street Doctor:**
                    Mobile Medicine for the Homeless 149
Thomas Scott and the St. Clare Medical Outreach

Chapter Thirteen **Student Aid:**
                      A Million Mentors Make Their Mark 161
Bill Gibbons and HOSTS (Help One Student To Succeed)

Chapter Fourteen **Preventative Maintenance** 173
Daniel Dominguez and the Christian Family Center

Chapter Fifteen **Keeping America Family-Friendly** 185
Tom Mason and Focus on the Family

A Final Word **Six Action Steps to Get Personally Involved** . . .195
Contact Information 200
Notes 203

Preface

PRESIDENT GEORGE W. BUSH has often stressed the importance of social entrepreneurs and faith-based initiatives to the health of America. Management expert Peter Drucker agrees, saying of social entrepreneurship:

> First, it's as important as economic entrepreneurship. More important, perhaps. In the United States, we have a very healthy economy but a very sick society. So perhaps social entrepreneurship is what we need the most—in health care, education, city government, and so on. Fortunately there are enough successes around so that we know it can be done—and also how to do it.[1]

The "successes" featured in this book serve ministries and organizations that are making a difference in millions of lives at home and abroad. These social entrepreneurs (SEs) come from a variety of backgrounds and represent a spectrum of social/spiritual concerns, from prison reform to higher education to medical care for the homeless. They are motivated by a love for Jesus Christ and a desire to live out the implications of His gospel. The essence of their sacrificial sharing is captured in a true story related by Anne Lamott in *Bird by Bird*.

> An eight-year-old boy had a younger sister who was dying of leukemia, and he was told that without a blood transfusion she would die. His parents explained to him that his blood was probably compatible with hers, and if so, he could be the blood donor. They asked him if they could test his blood. He said sure. So they did and it was a good match. Then they asked if he would give his sister a pint of blood, that it could be her only chance of living. He said he would have to think about it overnight.
>
> The next day he went to his parents and said he was willing to donate the blood. So they took him to the hospital

where he was put on a gurney beside his six-year-old sister. Both of them were hooked up to IVs. A nurse withdrew a pint of blood from the boy, which was then put in the girl's IV. The boy lay on his gurney in silence while the blood dripped into his sister, until the doctor came over to see how he was doing. Then the boy opened his eyes and asked, "How soon until I start to die?"[2]

"Greater love has no one than this," said Jesus, "that he lay down his life for his friends" (John 15:13). These SEs are laying down their lives daily for friends and strangers. In telling their unique stories we have highlighted universal principles in the hopes of educating and inspiring the rest of us to use our resources, abilities, and influence to create positive social change.

Our special thanks to Christy Merfeld, who transcribed hours of taped conversations. Thanks, too, to Kent Wilson, Greg Clouse, and the people at NavPress for seeing the potential in this book. Finally, we want to thank the contributors for their time and candor. They would like nothing better than for readers to contact them about their work. We would like nothing better than for readers to emulate these role models in making the future a brighter place for the less fortunate.

Merrill J. Oster
Mike Hamel

Bob Buford is a graduate of the University of Texas and is the former chairman of Buford Television, Inc. He has held leadership roles with Young Presidents Organization and World Presidents Organization and is well known as a leading social entrepreneur. Bob has founded or cofounded such organizations as Leadership Network, The Peter F. Drucker Foundation for Nonprofit Management, and HalfTime.

He is the author of three best-selling books: *Halftime*, *Game Plan*, and *Stuck in Halftime*. Bob and his wife, Linda, have been married since 1961. They make their home in Dallas and at Still Point Farm near Tyler, Texas.

RULES OF ENGAGEMENT

Bob Buford and the age of social entrepreneurs

"Social entrepreneur: A nonprofit-sector leader who attempts to address a social problem using private-sector strategies and tools."

Heather R. McLeod [1]

Few people know more about social entrepreneurs than Bob Buford, who in many ways is the prototype of this modern hybrid. He is the former chairman of Buford Television, Inc., a successful cable television company he ran for thirty years and sold in 1999. Today he spends his time, talent, and resources on a series of social ventures, including: Leadership Network, which serves more than fifteen thousand church leaders; The Peter F. Drucker Foundation for Nonprofit Management, which helps the social sector achieve excellence in performance and build responsible citizenship; and HalfTime (formerly FaithWorks), which helps business and professional leaders move from success to significance.

Bob describes himself as, "An entrepreneur at heart. Whether I express this in a business context or in the social sector, I think and act as an entrepreneur. In 1800, the word was defined by French economist Jean Baptiste Say as 'someone who takes resources from a state of lower to a state of higher yield and productivity.' A social entrepreneur does this in the social sector."

There have always been social entrepreneurs, but certain cultural trends have created a new and numerous breed of do-gooder. Buford labels the first of these trends, "the AOL opportunity: 'A' being *affluence*, 'O' being *options*, and 'L' being *longevity*.

Affluence has enabled many people at a certain point in their lives to do something other than income-producing work and consumption. The options available to them have been greatly increased by the demographic and economic changes in the western world. Life expectancy was around fifty years at the beginning of the twentieth century. At the start of the twenty-first century, the leading edge of the baby boom generation is cresting at fifty-five to sixty, and they still have a good twenty to twenty-five years to live. Most boomers don't know what to do with themselves, and many are discovering that becoming social entrepreneurs is the best option for their second half.

"Another cultural dynamic contributing to the proliferation of social entrepreneurs (SEs)," Bob continues, "is the heightened fear of aging and dying. Americans are desperately afraid of old age and of losing their potency and health. People are in denial of death. Jesus said the only way to save your life is to lose it (see Matthew 16:25-26). This truth often hits home during midlife. People realize that after all their acquiring and achieving and looking out for number one, the only way they can really 'get a life' is to give it away.

"A third factor catalyzing the social entrepreneurial movement has been a shift in the concept of success. Success in America has usually been defined in terms of money, fame, and power. Most adults allocate 90 percent of their energies to these Big Three on the 'Success Scale.' What drives a person to become a social entrepreneur is seeing the shallowness of this materialistic value system and switching to the 'Significance Scale,' which is calibrated to serving others instead of self. People who become SEs are looking for life, liberty, and the pursuit of blessedness—not happiness—and I believe the only way to be blessed is by being a blessing to others.

"The form this service takes for each person usually grows out of something that has been in their life a long, long time," Bob explains. "In my case I was given the gift of faith as a child and the question I always wrestled with was not, 'what I believed,' but, 'what would I do about what I believed.' In the first half of my life I was fairly limited because my energy went into my family and my work. The service outlets for me consisted of teaching a Bible class at my local church and investing in my marriage and my son. This is the norm for most of us. Then around midlife we begin to listen to the melody that's been playing in the background for years. What brought my interest in being a social entrepreneur to center stage was simply that I reached and exceeded my goals. And with my first-half objectives met, I could give myself more fully to serving God. This desire had been there all along, but I didn't feel that I could shift the balance in my life to do much about it before."

The apostle Paul tells Timothy to counsel believers,

> who are rich in this present world not to be arrogant nor to put their hope in wealth, which is so uncertain, but to put their hope in God, who richly provides us with every-thing for our enjoyment. Command them to do good, to be rich in good deeds, and to be generous and willing to share. In this way they will lay up treasure for themselves as a firm foundation for the coming age, so that they may take hold of the life that is truly life (1 Timothy 6:17-19).

Buford knows firsthand how difficult it can be to transition from success to significance. What he's learned through experi-ence and research has benefited the thousands who have heard him speak or read his books, the most well known of which is *Halftime: Changing Your Game Plan from Success to Significance*. Two sequels, *Game Plan: Winning Strategies for the Second Half of Your Life* and *Stuck in Halftime: Reinvesting Your One and Only Life* (Harper Collins/Zondervan), have also had a profound impact on a generation of SEs. His core insights can be distilled into half a dozen rules of engagement that will help potential and profes-sional SEs make the journey more effectively.

FIRST RULE: *GET INVOLVED IN WHAT GOD IS DOING.*
This first rule speaks to the foundational motivation of many SEs like Buford himself. His lifestyle grows out of his relationship with

God and is informed by the Bible. "Each of us is going to give an account to God," he says. "This final exam will have only two questions: 'What did you do with Jesus?' and 'What did you do with what I gave you?' The parable of the talents teaches with clarity that each of us has been given a certain mix of gifts and abilities to work with. At the end of the game we'll have to give an account of our stewardship.

"Arguably all Christians are called to some form of social entrepreneurship," Buford says. "Scripture summons us not only to a life of belief and worship, but to a life of faith and love. God told Adam and Eve to be fruitful and multiply. They weren't to bask in paradise and just live for themselves; they were to become parents of a great tribe. The Bible is full of people living out their faith in service. From their examples we learn that things go better if we join God in what He's doing rather than in originating something on our own."

Our "response"-ability is to respond to what God is doing, as best-selling author and teacher Henry Blackaby explains in *Experiencing God*:

> God takes the initiative to involve His people with Him in His work. He does this on His timetable, not on ours. He is the One who is already at work in our world. When He opens your spiritual eyes to see where He is at work, that revelation is your invitation to join Him. You will know where He is working when you see Him doing things that only God can do. When God reveals His work to you, that is the time He wants you to begin adjusting to Him and His activity.[2]

"Look out the window and see what's trying to happen whether or not you're involved with it," counsels Buford, "and then find a way to help."

SECOND RULE: *OPERATE OUT OF YOUR OWN HISTORY.*

The importance of this rule is self-evident in that, as Bob likes to say, "You can't give away what you don't have. I seldom meet a social entrepreneur whose success hasn't grown out of his or her prior history. One reason for the tremendous impact of the latest class of SEs is that they're not leaving behind their business skill-sets when they cross over to the social sector. They see a social or spiritual opportunity and organize themselves in a businesslike way to address the challenge.

"What we are most effective at," Bob notes, "will be reflected in our life experiences. It's a key indicator of where and how we should be serving. That's why a potential SE who is considering a new venture should take a fearless inventory of what he or she brings to the party. For me, I've always had a deep interest in man-agement and organization. This interest has been reflected in the organizations I've managed or started. My other passion is help-ing people move from success to significance in the second half of their lives, which has led to HalfTime."

The longer you live, the easier it should be to distinguish what you do abysmally, what you do adequately, and what you do admirably. Your goal should be to shift your efforts toward the prolific end of the continuum and avoid settling into the median of mediocrity.

THIRD RULE: *BEGIN WITH A PARALLEL CAREER.*

"The social entrepreneur changes the performance capacity of soci-ety," says Bob's friend Peter Drucker. "Clearly the need is there, or we wouldn't have founded 800,000 nonprofits over the past thirty years. Yesterday charity meant writing out a check. Today more and more people who are reasonably successful don't feel that's enough. They are looking for a parallel career, not a second career. Very few of them change jobs."[3]

Bob concurs. "The most effective SEs don't just quit their day jobs and jump into the abyss. They test their way in, often by run-ning low-cost probes to find out the nature of this new environ-ment called 'church' or 'hospital' or 'community organization.' They adopt a beginner's mindset and start small. More important, they start in the present instead of waiting until retirement or until all their ducks are in a row. They begin as amateurs and learn what they need to know about a possible second career while they still have cash flow from the first. I started Leadership Network in 1984, but I didn't sell my company until 1999, meaning I had parallel careers for fifteen years."

One further piece of advice from Buford on moving into the social arena: "You can dramatically accelerate your progress if you don't try to learn everything from scratch. Look for the kind of people I call 'translators.' These are bilingual experts who speak the language of two different cultures and can translate the social and economic distinctives from one to the other."

Fourth rule: *Envision an alternative future.*

Jim Collins, coauthor of *Build to Last*, coined a word in that book that has made its way into modern business parlance. A "BHAG" is a **B**ig, **H**airy, **A**udacious **G**oal. "Jim has described the concept to me in this way," Bob says. "He pictures three overlapping circles with BHAG written in their overlapping centers. One circle represents something you are very passionate about, something that grows out of your personal values. The second circle represents something at which you are the best in the world. I would say it's something you're supremely gifted to do. And the third circle has to do with what drives your economic engine."

The main benefit of a BHAG, according to Collins, is to inspire and focus organizations on achieving long-term objectives that are consistent with its purpose. One of the most famous BHAGs was the goal of landing a man on the moon before 1970....Your own BHAG need not be as dramatic as a moon landing, Collins says, but it should have the same traits characterized by Kennedy's vision. Aside from audacity, a good BHAG should meet three criteria:

1. It should have an extensive time frame, ranging from 10 to 30 years.

2. It should be clear, compelling, and easily expressed in plain English.
3. The BHAG should be consistent with your company's values and purpose.[4]

"A BHAG should be something that will transcend your lifetime," Bob adds. "It's got to be such a big piece of work that you can't finish it, an impossible dream that's more or less undoable without God's help. Whether it will carry on after you're gone has a lot to do with how well organized you are."

FIFTH RULE: *BUILD A TEAM TO ACCOMPLISH THE TASK.*

One of Peter Drucker's favorite aphorisms is, "All work is work for a team." There is no such thing as individual work. Even Jesus worked with the disciples. "In life when anyone accomplishes major objectives," says Zig Ziglar, "you can know that a 'team' helped him. In other words, when you see a turtle on a fence post, you can know he didn't get there by himself."[5]

Buford says in the acknowledgments for *Halftime,*

In the process of working on this book and on reviewing the facts of my life, I discovered a marvelous truth; I have never done anything important outside the context of a team. I think God must laugh at the seeming independence of us human beings who have such a tendency toward hubris and self-sufficiency. This may come from having made a lot of money, earning acclaim in sports, writing a book, or accomplishing something else extraordinary. God finds ways to teach all of us who are puffed up with ourselves how interdependent we really are.[6]

Buford then quotes one of his favorite passages from Scripture affirming the need for appropriate humility and proper dependence on God and others.

Do not think of yourself more highly than you ought, but rather think of yourself with sober judgment, in accordance with the measure of faith God has given you. Just as each of us has one body with many members, and these members do not all have the same function, so in Christ we who are many form one body, and each member belongs to all the others. We have different gifts, according to the grace given us (Romans 12:3-6).

SIXTH RULE: *PERSIST THROUGH ADVERSITY OVER TIME.*

"Most people who choose a career in business realize they need to go to college and serve an apprenticeship of some duration to learn the specifics of an industry," Bob observes. "Yet when it comes to a second career in the social sector, they expect it to be easier. That's not how it works. SEs aren't exempt from the learning curve or from paying the 'dumb tax' charged for learning any new business. This is one reason more people don't become successful social entrepreneurs—they quit when they realize that *all* work is hard work. However, the good ones accept this and persist."

"The race is not always to the swift," says inventor Richard C. Levy, "but to those who keep running. It is a mistake to think anything is made overnight, other than baked goods and newspapers. Levy's first corollary is: Nothing is as easy as it looks. Levy's second corollary is: Everything takes longer than you think." By way of illustration, he tells the following story of Norm Larsen:

> When the Convair Co. could not find a way to stop San Diego's night fog from rusting Atlas missile parts they were manufacturing, it put out a public plea for assistance. Norm Larsen, a local chemist, responded with 39 formulas. But it was his 40th that held the answer, producing a petroleum-based chemical that gets under water and displaces it through the pores of metal. Larsen's invention became WD-40. ...By the way, in case you have ever wondered what WD-40 stands for, it is "Water Displacement–40th formula."[7]

"Get used to disappointment," is what the Dread Pirate Roberts tells his true love, Buttercup, in *The Princess Bride*. This is wise counsel for people who want to become social entrepreneurs. "Going from success to significance is hard work," Bob insists.

"There are innumerable moments of doubt and uncertainty. Noah must have wondered if it was ever going to rain. Abraham certainly had second thoughts as he trekked around the Promised Land. Joshua probably felt nervous on the sixth trip around Jericho. It's the same with all those who follow God's calling, especially SEs. Their efforts aren't recognized and appreciated as they were in their former careers. They run into delays and obstacles they never expected.

"There are two kinds of opposition," Bob says, "the 'in-your-face' frontal kind, and what some call 'conservative opposition.' Conservative opposition is the toughest to detect and deal with. Let me tell you a story: When I was in the subscription television business, I once called on the general manager of the Cincinnati Reds. On the way to his office at the ballpark, I noticed they served Oscar Meyer top-quality wieners. Thinking that less expensive hotdogs would do just as well, I asked the GM why the extra expense. He said, 'The fans know the difference. They don't tell us. They just don't come back—and they tell their neighbors.' That's what I mean by conservative opposition. It's where others just don't go along with your program. Something doesn't work and it's the kind of thing where you never quite know what hit you."

Bob Buford's insights are validated by the stories of the other social entrepreneurs in this book. While their fields of endeavor vary widely, the following chart shows just how similar their experiences are. The path from success to significance is well worn. It's not that hard to find, but it will take everything you have to follow.

FOR MORE INFORMATION, CONTACT
Leadership Network, or, HalfTime
2501 Cedar Springs, Suite 200
Dallas, TX 75201
214-979-2431 (Leadership Network)
www.leadnet.org
214-720-0878 (HalfTime)
www.halftime.org

BOOKS THAT HAVE INFLUENCED BOB BUFORD
The Success Syndrome: Hitting Bottom When You Reach the Top, Steven Berglas, New York: Da Capo Press, 1986.

Managing the Nonprofit Organization: Principles and Practices, Peter F. Drucker, New York: Harper Business, 1992.

Real Power: Stages of Personal Power in Organizations, Janet O. Hagberg, Salem, Wis.: Sheffeld Publishing, 1993.

Transitions: Making Sense of Life's Changes, William Bridges, Cambridge, Mass.: Perseus, 1980.

The Hungry Spirit: Beyond Capitalism, Charles Handy, New York: Broadway Books, 1999.

	Follows God's initiative	Operates from personal history	Parallel career	Sees alternate future	Builds a team	Overcomes adversity
Ken Blanchard	X	X	X	X	X	
Juan Benitez	X	X		X	X	
Glen Kehrein	X	X		X	X	X
Linc Washington	X	X		X	X	X
Elayne Bennett	X	X		X	X	
David Burdine	X	X		X	X	X
Jerry Wilger	X	X		X	X	
Duncan Campbell	X	X	X	X	X	X
Sean Lambert	X	X		X	X	X
Kit Danley	X	X		X	X	X
Larry Donnithorne	X	X		X	X	
Fred Peterson	X	X		X	X	X
Thomas Scott	X	X	X	X	X	
Bill Gibbons	X	X	X	X	X	X
Daniel Dominguez	X	X	X	X	X	X
Tom Mason	X	X		X	X	X

Ken Blanchard is the Chief Spiritual Officer of The Ken Blanchard Companies and the cofounder of The Center for *Faith*Walk Leadership. He is a past recipient of the National Speakers Association's *Council of Peers Award of Excellence* and the *Golden Gavel Award* from Toastmasters International. He is a visiting lecturer at his alma mater, Cornell University, where he also serves as a trustee emeritus.

The One Minute Manager, which Blanchard coauthored with Spencer Johnson, has sold more than ten million copies and is one of the most successful business books of all time. He has coauthored twenty other books. Ken and Margie Blanchard have been married forty years. They have two grown children—who work in the family business—and two grandchildren. The Blanchards make their home in San Diego, California.

Chapter One

Follow the (Servant) Leader

Ken Blanchard and The Center for *Faith*Walk Leadership

"Tell me who your admired leaders are, and you have bared your soul."

Garry Wills[1]

Not all social entrepreneurs work with people who are on the bottom of the pile. Some focus on the folks occupying the top rungs on the ladder of success, believing that if you can change a leader, you can change a company, a culture, or a country. One such optimist is world-renowned business consultant Ken Blanchard. These days he is taking a radical approach to leadership based on over thirty years of research and his own personal encounter with the greatest leader of all time.

Along with his friend Phil Hodges, Ken has started The Center for *Faith*Walk Leadership, which promotes servant leadership based on the teachings and example of Jesus Christ. This model isn't just for churches and nonprofits, but for marketplace organizations of all shapes and sizes. Ken shares with executives as well as pastors a message that has transformed his own life and leadership style.

ON THE VERGE

Ken attended Cornell University, where he met and married Marjorie McKee. Both eventually became college professors. However, their teaching and communication abilities would not remain confined to the classroom. "While on sabbatical in 1979," Ken remembers, "we were invited to a YPO (Young Presidents Organization) University in Hawaii. On Monday I taught a session on leadership and about 250 of the 1,200 attendees came. Two days later I did a session on motivation with about 700 in attendance. Friday's session drew the whole conference.

"Some of the people asked what I planned to do after my sabbatical. 'Going back to the university,' I replied. They said, 'You're crazy! When you're hot, you're hot. Start your own company.' I told them I couldn't even balance my checkbook, how could I start my own company? They said, 'We'll help you.' And so, five YPOers helped Margie and me start Blanchard Training and Development. When *The One Minute Manager* hit bookstores in 1982 the phones began ringing off their hooks. The book made the bestsellers' list in less than a week. It never budged for three years. It was crazy. We almost went under because so many things came at us all at once. That's when I started asking myself what the Lord was doing."

Ken told Stephen Caldwell of *Life@Work* magazine:

It struck me that I was either going to get a big head or I was going to find out what was going on. It was too incredible to take credit for. . . .Several months after the book was out, I got a call from Phil Hodges, a longtime friend from Cornell, wanting to know if we could get together. . . .That meeting with Phil Hodges marked the renewal of my spiritual journey that had begun when I was a little guy being taken to church by my parents. Afterward, Phil kept calling me, sending me things to read, pushing me to think about my relationship with Christ.[2]

"About this time, I ran into Bob Buford going to a YPO University in Mexico," Blanchard continues. "On the flight, we talked about God and Christianity. At the end of the trip, Bob said, 'I'm going to turn you over to a friend of mine named Bill Hybels who will be in Mexico City.' When I met Hybels, he told me several helpful things, including the difference between religion and Christianity. 'Religion is spelled d-o, Christianity is spelled d-o-n-e.' My lunch with Bill really made me think, but I wasn't ready to suit up yet.

"About a year later," he recalls, "Margie and I were facing a problem in the company. We'd turned the presidency over to a man we later found out was doing some things that were inconsistent with what we believed. One evening we met for dinner to decide what to do. On the drive to the restaurant I finally got it! 'Blanchard,' I told myself, 'you're trying to do this by yourself.' Hybels had told me earlier that if I signed on as a Christian, I'd get three consultants for the price of one. I would get the Father who started it, the Son who lived it, and the Holy Spirit who is the day-to-day operational manager. I bowed my head in the car and told the Lord, 'I can't do this by myself. I need you.'"

> *Many social entrepreneurs develop parallel careers, starting a new venture while still in their old jobs.*

Margie and the children noticed the difference in Ken almost immediately and it had a spiritual impact on them. "Margie is much more thoughtful than I am," says Ken. "With Phil's help, she came to her own commitment to Christ a few years later, and our kids are moving along in their own ways."

OVER THE TOP

As new believers become more concerned about building God's kingdom than their own, they begin looking for ways to serve. For some this involves moving into a new job or ministry. Many social entrepreneurs develop parallel careers, starting a new venture while still in their old jobs. Ken has followed this pattern, launching The Center for *Faith*Walk Leadership without leaving his company. He has reoriented his role there, however. "I changed my title to Chief Spiritual Officer," he explains with a smile. "I make it part of my job to keep the energy and spirit up among our staff of 250. One thing

I do is a morning devotional on voicemail. Initially some people resented it. They thought I was pushing religion. So I made a deal with them. If I planned to get really Christian, I'd say so up front so they could turn it off if they didn't want to listen.

"When I turned sixty in 1999, I celebrated for about six weeks. I was very excited about it. I felt my first fifty-nine years had been preparation for the next thirty-five or forty. One of my projects became talking Bill Hybels and Phil Hodges into writing *Leadership by the Book*. While working on the book, we came up with the idea of creating The Center for *Faith*Walk Leadership. I got a sense that this was my mission, my ministry. We launched the Center as a nonprofit entity later that year with the goal of challenging and equipping people to lead like Jesus."

The vision of the center is "to see a growing community of people effectively serving in strategic leadership roles who have surrendered their ambitions, thoughts, and behaviors to the daily guidance of the Holy Spirit. We want to help leaders walk their faith and apply the leadership genius of Jesus to their own organizations," says the ministry's cofounder. "Although many people identify with Jesus as Lord and Savior, they don't see Him as a viable model for leadership. But in His training of the disciples, Jesus exemplified the heart, mind, and methods of a servant leader, and produced extraordinary results with ordinary people."

"You know that the rulers of the Gentiles lord over them," Jesus told His handpicked trainees, "and their high officials exercise authority over them. Not so with you. Instead, whoever wants to become great among you must be your servant, and whoever wants to be first must be your slave—just as the Son of Man did not come to be served, but to serve, and to give his life as a ransom for many" (Matthew 20:25-28).

The optimal phrase is "not so with you." Jesus intended something quite different from what the disciples were familiar with. However, just believing in the concept doesn't make one a servant leader. "Some leaders can use service as a means to ego-driven ends," Ken warns. "They serve to accumulate power, recognition, and control. Eventually they no longer serve people, but have people serve them. The key to a servant leader's heart is humility. People with humility don't think less of themselves, they just think of themselves less."

In their book *The Power of Ethical Management*, Norman Vincent Peale and Blanchard suggest that it's healthy to feel good about yourself. "But don't get carried away," Ken adds. "Watch out for the ego. Someone once told me that ego stands for 'Edging God Out.' When we get a distorted image of our own importance and see ourselves as the center of the universe, we lose touch with who we really are as children of God. Our thinking blurs. We lose the sense of our connection with others and with our true selves.

"There are two types of ego-centeredness: *self-doubt* and *false pride*. Both are enemies of humility. People with self-doubt are consumed with their shortcomings and tend to be hard on themselves. People with false pride think they don't need grace and are out of touch with their own vulnerability to sinfulness. Both have a hard time believing that they are loved."[3]

The key to a servant leader's heart is humility. People with humility don't think less of themselves, they just think of themselves less.

Effective social entrepreneurs are humble servant leaders with a clear vision of what needs doing. Servant leadership isn't an oxymoron. Humility and vision aren't mutually exclusive. The first is the fulcrum while the latter is the lever that moves people. "Servant leadership starts with vision," Ken insists. "Vision sees a picture of the future that creates a passion people will follow. A clear vision has four aspects:

Purpose. This defines what business we're in.
Image. This pictures how things would look if everything ran as planned.
Values. These determine how we should behave when working on our purpose.
Goals. These focus our energies on the here-and-now.

"Once the vision is clear, the next aspect of leadership is implementation—how you live according to the vision. During implementation, the traditional pyramid has to be turned upside down and the leader has to demonstrate different behavior. This is where real servant leadership behaviors begin. For example, servant leaders have to listen more than talk. They have to share credit. They have to be open to feedback. Self-serving leaders hate feedback. Servant leaders love it because their objective is not to protect their position but to serve."

"Because leadership is necessarily an exercise or authority," says Eugene Peterson in his introduction to 2 Corinthians in *The Message*, "it easily shifts into an exercise of power. But the minute it does that, it begins to inflict damage on both the leader and the led. Paul, studying Jesus, had learned a kind of leadership in which he managed to stay out of the way so that the others could deal with God without having to go through him."[4]

Ken is quick to dispel some misconceptions about servant leadership. "Don't make the mistake of assuming this means letting the inmates run the prison. Servant leaders don't relinquish responsibility or try to please everyone. Jesus certainly didn't. He only sought to please the vision He got from the top of the hierarchy. Vision always comes from the top. That doesn't mean you don't involve others in developing it, but the responsibility lies with the head of the organization, division, department, or family.

"Neither is servant leadership a soft management concept. In fact, effective servant leaders create organizations that have a sound, triple bottom line: raving-fan customers, gung ho people, and financial well-being. These are the payoffs for a company— or a ministry—led by someone committed to following the head, heart, and hands of Jesus-like leadership."

When asked if people who are not followers of Jesus can be involved with the Center, Blanchard answers with an enthusiastic, "Absolutely! But they must be clear that our model for leadership is Jesus Christ and that the management text we use is the Bible." The Center helps strategic leaders develop the skills and behaviors required for servant leadership. In addition, they also provide personalized consulting to top leaders who want to implement servant leadership practices in their organizations. This focus on the top comes from Blanchard's long consulting experience, which has taught him that significant change in organizational culture only occurs when top management is fully committed to it.

WHAT NEXT?

Blanchard has discovered that many successful leaders are asking, "What's next?" They are financially secure and recognized as high achievers. They have a certain amount of power and status. Now they want to know, "Where do I go from here?"

At this point in their careers, some people shift to the social sector and become full-time social entrepreneurs. Others, like Ken himself, prefer to live and work in both worlds. "The one concern I have about people switching to the social sector," he says, "is that some of them leave miserable messes behind. They would be better off changing themselves rather than their settings. I'm interested in helping people move from success to significance where they are.

True heroism is...not the urge to surpass all others at whatever cost, but the urge to serve others at whatever cost.

"Through The *Faith*Walk Center, we enable people to achieve a sense of greater significance by becoming servant leaders. We equip them to make their current organizations their personal *Faith*Walk ministry. In other words, they stay put and serve. They change their job descriptions, but not their jobs. They get interested in moving from self-serving leadership to servant leadership."

"Strength is for service, not status," says the apostle Paul. "Each one of us needs to look after the good of the people around us, asking ourselves, 'How can I help?'" (Romans 15:1-2, MSG). Conventional wisdom says nice guys who put others first finish last in sports, in business, and in life. "So many of us think life is all about winning," Ken points out, "but I like the words of the late tennis star Arthur Ashe: 'True heroism is remarkably sober, very undramatic. It's not the urge to surpass all others at whatever cost, but the urge to serve others at whatever cost.'"

Although he is the coauthor of twenty books, the most powerful words Ken has written have not been widely read yet. They come from his own obituary, which reads in part,

> Ken Blanchard was a loving teacher and example of simple truths whose books and lectures on leadership and management helped himself and others awaken the presence of God in their lives....He was someone who trusted God's unconditional love and believed he was *the beloved*. He valued integrity and walked his talk....He will be missed because wherever he went he made the world a better place for his having been there.[5]

"Death is a strip search," says author Gregg Levoy. "It points the barrel of mortality at your head and demands to see what you have hidden under your garments."[6] "When you write your obituary," says the energetic Blanchard, who is very much alive, "it's a dream, a big-picture goal of what you want your life to be. Through The Center for *Faith*Walk Leadership, I am challenging myself and other leaders to look ahead—over the horizon—and lead the way beyond success to significance."

Givers and Receivers
Jim Mudd Sr.

I AM THE PRESIDENT AND CEO of a large advertising firm that works with automobile dealers across North America. Before meeting Ken Blanchard, I had been impacted by his writings in such books as *Raving Fans* and *Gung Ho*. I bought a copy of the latter for each of my employees and adopted its tenets, which improved both morale and profitability.

Ken's books, as well as others such as *Business as a Calling* by Michael Novak, inspired me to believe that God wanted me to serve Him in the full-time ministry of my business. I felt Him asking me to use my gifts to lift people up and encourage them to become all He wanted them to be. However, I didn't know how to live out this inspiration. Then I met Ken at a business meeting in California and received a personal invitation to an upcoming *Faith*Walk conference. At the conference, God used Ken and his colleague Phil Hodges to give me the step-by-step instruction I needed. Jesus' admonition to servant leadership in Matthew 20:25-28 particularly touched me. I came away impressed with the importance of turning the leadership pyramid upside down and of what Ken calls a "trickle-up" philosophy instead of the usual "top-down" approach to management.

I am a raving fan of *Faith*Walk because it has drawn me closer to Jesus Christ and has given me a practical way to express my faith at work. The ministry has helped me understand Jesus' philosophies and model them in a way that doesn't turn people off. It's given me a clearer understanding of scriptural principles and how to apply them in a business environment. I am better able to experience and explain the awesome power our Savior wants to have in our lives.

I believe Blanchard has a special anointing to help people like me find the way to live as followers of Jesus in the marketplace. Ken has always been a very dynamic communicator, but he is even more animated and powerful now as he talks about Jesus Christ as *the* model for leadership.

Perhaps that's because he's practicing what he preaches.

FOR MORE INFORMATION, CONTACT
The Center for *Faith*Walk Leadership
125 State Place
Escondido, CA 92029
800-728-6000
www.faithwalkleadership.com

BOOKS THAT HAVE INFLUENCED KEN BLANCHARD
Leadership Is an Art, Max De Pree, New York: Dell, 1990.
Halftime: Changing Your Game Plan from Success to Significance, Bob Buford, Grand Rapids, Mich.: Zondervan, 1994.
The Soul of the Firm, C. William Pollard, New York: HarperBusiness, 1996.
Ordering Your Private World, Gordon MacDonald, Nashville: Oliver Nelson, 1984.
The Divine Conspiracy: Rediscovering Our Hidden Life in God, Dallas Willard, San Francisco: HarperCollins, 1998.

Juan Benitez was born and raised in Cuba. He came to the United States in 1965 as a sixteen-year-old political refugee. He graduated from the University of Missouri in 1972 with a B.S. in mechanical engineering. In 1980 he joined the founding team for Micron Technology and became company president five years later. He joined the first Bush administration in 1989 as a deputy assistant secretary of commerce and later served as deputy undersecretary of commerce for technology. Juan has also served on blue-ribbon government panels and testified before Congress on several occasions.

Since 1998, Juan has served as president and CEO of Enterprise Development International. He and his wife have one adult son. They make their home in Warrenton, Virginia.

Chapter Two

CAPITAL IDEA: GETTING THE MOST FOR YOUR MONEY

Juan Benitez and Enterprise Development International

"All they asked was that we should continue to remember the poor, the very thing I was eager to do."

Paul the apostle[1]

Jesus stated the obvious when he told His disciples, "The poor you will always have with you, and you can help them any time you want" (Mark 14:7). And from then until now, Christians have been in the forefront of caring for the world's destitute and disenfranchised. Hospitals, orphanages, schools, rescue missions, homeless shelters, and other expressions of humanitarian concern have either been started or improved by conscientious believers.

This same practical love has found economic expression through programs that enable people in poverty to rise to a level of self-sufficiency. One of the most effective is Enterprise Development International. EDI provides business training and small business loans to low-income people with viable ideas. Since 1985 they have helped more than 100,000 such entrepreneurs—80 percent of whom are women—create more than 250,000 jobs in over fifty countries. They have mobilized and recirculated more than twenty million dollars and made a difference in the lives of over 800,000 people.

PAYBACK

The social entrepreneur running this innovative effort is Juan Benitez, a Cuban refugee and former deputy assistant secretary of commerce. Juan grew up under Castro. His father sent him to America as a political refugee when Juan was sixteen. He lived with his brother and other refugees in a housing project in Kansas City, Missouri, and put himself through high school and the University of Missouri by working three or four jobs at a time, doing everything from cleaning toilets to making tortillas. He graduated in 1972 with a degree in mechanical engineering and went to work for General Motors.

Juan migrated from there to the high-tech industry. In 1980 he joined a start-up called Micron Technology and became responsible for designing and building their manufacturing facility to produce computer memory chips. The company survived some rough times and did very well. So did Juan, who became president of Micron at the end of 1985. By the time he left three years later, Micron's annual revenues had reached three hundred million dollars.

As Juan grew personally and professionally, he developed a strong sense of payback. "I wanted to show my appreciation to God for everything He had done," he says. "I also wanted to give something back to this wonderful country for being so good to me. And so I retired from Micron in 1988 and got involved in politics, starting with the first George Bush campaign." After the election, Benitez was appointed deputy assistant secretary of commerce for science and electronics. Later he became deputy undersecretary of technology at the Commerce Department. When he finished his government stint, Juan returned to the private sector. However, the nagging sense that he should be doing more with his life wouldn't go away. He spent more than a year working with Opportunity International before becoming president and CEO of a similar work, Enterprise Development International, in March of 1998.

You and I are the callees and God is the Call-er. God equips the worker and assigns the work.

His move from the corporate to the nonprofit sector cost Juan a handsome salary. He went from earning big bucks to trying to raise them on behalf of others. Sometimes he wonders if he should have stayed a little longer in his corner office and earned a little more. "Hindsight is wonderful and I sometimes second-guess myself. I've been blessed in many ways and I'm very thankful for what I have. But a few years more in the corporate world would have given me a much higher financial capacity and I could be doing more today. It's a tough decision. People have to do what they do, when they do it, from a sense of calling."

Pastor and author John Ortberg explains a calling as:

> something you discover, not something you choose. The word *vocation* comes from the Latin word for voice. Discovering it involves very careful listening. People will sometimes speak about "choosing their calling," but a chosen calling is an oxymoron. The whole idea of a calling is taken from Scripture, where time after time God calls someone to do his work. The whole idea of calling is that there is a Call-er and a call-ee. You and I are the call-ees and God is the Call-er. God equips the worker and assigns the work.[2]

For Benitez, his sense of personal calling is crucial. "I believe strongly that God directs our lives and maps out our journeys. Look what He's done for me. I was born into a wealthy family. Overnight we became poor when Castro confiscated our businesses. I left my home and family and became the poorest of the poor—a refugee. Then God took me on a very steep success curve from minimum wage jobs to being the president of Micron. I've gone from wealth to poverty to wealth again, and from there into the nonprofit world. What a ride! And through it all, my sense of calling has given me direction and balance."

RETURN ON INVESTMENT

Juan laughs when he says, "Raising money is a lot harder than earning it, yet this is perhaps the most critical function of CEOs in nonprofit organizations. But securing capital is only half the battle; the organization also needs to get the maximum return on investment (ROI) in accomplishing its mission. And this is just where Enterprise excels."

EDI does not give handouts but makes loans to the working poor, a sizable group, according to The World Bank, which estimates that 1.3 billion people live on less than a dollar a day. A potential client has to have a viable idea or business concept to receive training and a loan. The low rate of interest charged for the money covers the operating cost of the local organization that administers the program. The principal is recycled as revolving loan funds in the program's own neighborhoods. It moves from one borrower to the next and helps each to build a livelihood. Repayment rates exceed 95 percent, far surpassing the performance of commercial institutions. From an annual budget of about 1.5 million dollars in 2001 they issued loans to over 33,000 clients totaling more than 4.4 million dollars. Their donor list includes corporations, foundations, churches, secular organizations, and some matching grants from the U.S. Agency for International Development.

Because capital is typically lent two-and-a-half times a year, a 600-dollar donation becomes five short-term loans of about 300 dollars each in just the first year. Over five years, that same donation finances twenty-five loans totaling nearly 7,500 dollars, and provides incomes for more than 125 people. Loan amounts depend on the local economy. The average loan in Manila is 25 dollars, in Romania it's 800 dollars, and in Mexico it's 250 dollars. EDI currently supports one domestic and twelve international programs. The main difference between developing-world and domestic programs is the cost. The average loan worldwide is 300 dollars, a substantial sum in many settings, but not in America.

Rather than cultivate dependency, EDI's strategy of micro-enterprise creates self-supporting entrepreneurs and, as a consequence, healthier families and stronger communities. "We can track the impact we are having on our clients," Benitez maintains. "We know their living conditions when they get their first loan and business training through our local programs. As they start and grow their businesses we can see the improvements. They are able to feed their families, live in better houses, send their kids to school, pay for medical and dental care—things we take for granted, but that were beyond reach for these folks before EDI."

In addition to Benitez, Enterprise has attracted a staff of other top-notch people who could be making a lot more money elsewhere. They share Juan's sense of calling and his motivation to serve Christ through serving the poor. The spiritual motivation behind the financial model goes all the way back to EDI's roots, planted by a missionary in East Africa named Paris Reidhead. Beyond evangelizing the poor, he wanted to help them improve their lives. With a group of prominent business and church leaders he established a nonprofit organization in the U.S. that eventually became EDI. Businessman Robert (Bud) Hancock served as the first executive director. Since its inception, Enterprise has had a strong board of directors comprised of committed businesspeople with a great passion for the work.

While Christianity motivates EDI, religion is never used as a screening device. Clients are selected and served regardless of race, gender, or creed. None of its programs impose religious requirements. "On the giving side, the majority of our individual donors are Christians," Juan says, "but they don't necessarily give to Enterprise because we take our mandate to help the poor from the Bible. We have a lot of folks who give because they like our model and the way we leverage their gifts for maximum effect."

"Inspiring trust is important for any organization," writes Robert Watson, former National Commander of The Salvation Army. "But it's life-and-death for a nonprofit. People invest their time and their money in institutions they believe to be honest and effective....When we asked people in the spring of 2000 to rank desirable attributes of charities, they rated 'uses donations effectively' as the most important consideration."[3]

SUSTAINABLE SOLUTIONS

Enterprise is all about bringing lasting changes to the lifestyles of the poor and overlooked, but good intent is never enough. There has to be a workable means to this worthy end. As Benitez sees it, one of the most fundamental aspects of EDI's approach is *sustainability*, meaning that its programs cover their own operating costs over time.

This is a no-brainer for Benitez, who says, "Given my business background, I've always believed firmly in sustainable solutions. Relief work is good. Helping the needy on a short-term basis certainly has its place. But addressing the long-term needs of the poor in self-sustaining ways is the key to improving their situation. Our programs generate enough revenues to cover their operating costs by the time they reach maturity. We keep overhead to a minimum. Instead of staffing our own branch offices around the world, we work closely with local organizations that understand the needs of their communities. We supply them with the training, business expertise, and capital they need, then ask them to concentrate on the poorest of the poor in their regions."

Doing business through affiliates has its challenges, especially when operating in the developing world. In many countries corruption and bribes are the norm. But not for Enterprise. "We wouldn't tolerate that," Juan insists. "We monitor our programs very closely. Every dollar has to be accounted for. If anything improper were being done, we would know it right away and put a stop to it. Our best safeguard against dishonesty is in partnering with committed Christians who are people of integrity. Certainly our clients—those who receive the monies—are exposed to graft and corruption; it's part of the environment in many places. That's why our training includes teaching people to do what's right and not cave in to the pressure."

Addressing the long-term needs of the poor in self-sustaining ways is the key to improving their situation.

Mother Teresa once told a group of western business people convened in New Delhi that, "If each one of you would use the same drive you use in building your business and use it to help others, just think what a force that would be and what a difference you could make for a better world for all." Juan Benitez wasn't part of that group, but he has responded to the challenge and proven the truth behind it. And he has some advice for those who might want to do the same.

"First," Juan says, "make sure the organization you start or serve has a good return on investment in the form of changed lives. Are their clients being transformed because of the services they provide? Next, make sure the specific programs and services are cost-effective and efficient. Check to see that things are being done according to sound business practices and that the organization has the necessary administrative, managerial, and financial skills to wisely handle the resources entrusted to them."

Make sure the organization you start or serve has a good return on investment in the form of changed lives.

This emphasis on outcomes is a distinctive of the new breed of social entrepreneurs like Benitez. Writing on the subject in *Inc.*, Heather McLeod says:

> For social entrepreneurs, market-based thinking has also created a greater focus on the organization's results than on its processes. "Before, we were like all the other social-service agencies; we looked less at outcomes and more at process," says Rick Aubry, executive director of Rubicon Programs Inc., a nonprofit in California...."We'd ask, 'How many people walked in the door?' instead of 'How many people are better off from having walked in the door?'"[4]

McLeod goes on to list some practical benefits of keeping outcomes in view: "It helps depoliticize social-services organizations by substituting concrete measurements for subjective interpretations. It also provides clear goals against which employees can measure their progress and accomplishments, a psychological blessing in a line of work that to employees often feels like shoveling sand uphill."[5]

Juan does indeed feel blessed. "I have been given so much—

good health, a great wife, a wonderful son and daughter-in-law, freedom, prosperity, I could go on and on. God has blessed me in so many ways. I ask Him every day to give me the wisdom and guidance I need to be a blessing to others, especially to the poor."

Givers and Receivers
In Romania

MARIANA HALGAS is a forty-five-year-old divorced mother of three. Trained as a teacher, she frequently has been unemployed. After completing the required business-training course offered by EDI's local partner organization, HIRO, Mariana received her first loan and launched a company providing housecleaning and child-care services. Soon, two of her daughters followed in her path and received training and loans for their own enterprises. "I wanted to regain my independence and to find myself after a long period of struggle, so I turned to HIRO," Mariana says. "I am confident that the money invested in the business will be recouped, and I already have a profit! The payoff also is spiritual and moral, as I was able to offer jobs to several women and even change the attitudes of my clients toward the women who worked for me. After all, house-keepers and babysitters are human, too."

In the Philippines

THE WIFE OF A CHICKEN FARMER and a mother of five, Teresita Rico has been a client of CCT, Enterprise Development's partner in the Philippines, since 1999. She has a grocery-delivery business in her neighborhood, selling sacks and cans of such staples as cooking oil and rice, along with various frozen foods. Teresita is now on her third loan, using the 10,000 pesos (about 200 dollars) to finance an increase in her inventory. "My income is up very big—three times what it was," she said, crediting her loan for the increase. The additional income helped make possible the adoption of an additional child—she has five of her own. Teresita plans to use a future loan to fund the purchase of a sewing machine that can produce a zigzag stitch, which she hopes to use to produce bed linens for sale.

In India

AT TWENTY-FIVE, Abul Hossen was a hardworking but desperate young man. To support his wife and two children, his best prospect was to rent a van rickshaw, or bicycle taxi, to pedal for hire. But when one was available at all, it cost a high rate of twenty rupees (about fifty cents) for just four hours. So Abul would be lucky to bring home a dollar a day, and often the family went hungry. Then Abul heard about Enterprise Development's partner program and was elated to learn that he was eligible to make payments on his own van rickshaw. He applied, and soon began the ten-month cycle of weekly, two-dollar payments. In the meantime, his income jumped to almost three dollars a day—enough to feed and clothe his family, send his children to school, and pay for incidental medical needs. After he paid off his loan, Abul's expendable income rose accordingly, and, most important, he retained possession of his first true working asset: his own bicycle taxi.

FOR MORE INFORMATION, CONTACT
Enterprise Development International
10395 Democracy Lane
Fairfax VA, 22030
800-936-2253
www.endpoverty.org

BOOKS THAT HAVE INFLUENCED JUAN BENITEZ
Mere Christianity, C. S. Lewis, New York: Macmillan, 1952.
Jesus/CEO: Using Ancient Wisdom for Visionary Leadership, Laurie Beth Jones, New York: Hyperion, 1995.
The Best and the Brightest: 20th Anniversary Edition, David Halberstam, New York: Random House, 2001.
A Prayer for Owen Meany, John Irving, New York: Random House, 1990.
The World Is My Home, James A. Michener, New York: Random House, 1992.

Glen Kehrein is the founder of Circle Urban Ministries on Chicago's west side, where he and his wife, Lonni, have lived for thirty years and raised their three kids. What began as a youth drop-in center has grown to become a national leader in urban community reclamation and development. Glen is the coauthor of the award-winning book, *Breaking Down Walls: A Model of Reconciliation in an Age of Racial Strife*, and has contributed to three other books. He holds a B.A. in Bible/theology from Moody Bible Institute and a B.A. in sociology from Wheaton College. In 1997 he became the first American to be awarded a doctorate of peacemaking from Westminster College for his efforts in racial reconciliation.

Abraham Lincoln Washington is senior pastor of Rock of Our Salvation Church. Prior to Rock, he served as senior pastor of Transformation Crusade Ministries for five years and as chaplain of Circle Urban Ministries for nine years. Before relocating his wife, Lisa, and three children to the Chicago area, Linc served as a pastor of evangelism and youth for eight years in Jacksonville, Florida, and as a prison ministry pastor for two years. His theological training includes two years at Philippian Institute of Biblical Studies in Jacksonville, and two years at Moody Bible Institute in Chicago.

Chapter Three

BEAUTY FROM ASHES: A MODEL FOR RACIAL RECONCILIATION

Glen Kehrein and Circle Urban Ministries

Abraham Lincoln Washington and Rock of Our Salvation Church

"Before the victory of brotherhood is achieved, some will maybe face physical death, but we shall overcome. Before the victory is won, some will lose jobs, some will be called communists, and reds, merely because they believe in brotherhood, some will be dismissed as dangerous rabble-rousers and agitators merely because they're standing up for what is right, but we shall overcome."

Martin Luther King Jr.[1]

For all our wealth and success, America is still plagued by large pockets of poverty inhabited by a permanent underclass. Many people, mostly minorities, are still trapped in desperate places where crime and drugs are rampant and fractured families and ruined lives are piled into demoralized communities. Such a community is Austin, on Chicago's west side, which the *Chicago Tribune* once called one of the city's most dangerous neighborhoods. But over the past quarter century it has slowly undergone a miraculous renovation from an urban wasteland into an oasis of hope. Residents have a better place to live and a brighter future because of the efforts of social entrepreneurs like Glen Kehrein, who moved into the area at the height of urban flight in 1973, and

"Linc" Washington. These two men, their families, and the organizations they serve have mobilized thousands of volunteers and brought beauty from ashes.

RENAISSANCE

Sparking this local renaissance has been the partnership between Circle Urban Ministries, which Glen started as a youth drop-in center, and Rock of Our Salvation Church, now pastored by Abraham Lincoln Washington. Like the Kehreins, the Washingtons had moved into the community, where for nine years prior to becoming pastor of Rock Church, Linc served as chaplain of Circle Urban Ministries.

Faith-based partnerships are a powerful force for urban renewal when they unite the church and parachurch in a common cause. The alliance between Circle Urban and Rock Church is a model of community reclamation that enriches the lives of over 13,000 Austin residents annually through various programs, many of which are based out of a five-building complex anchored by a 150,000-square-foot building that was once an epicenter of crime and drug traffic. The fledgling ministry bought an old school complex from the Chicago Board of Education in 1984 for 80,000 dollars. Later they purchased two adjacent and abandoned apartment buildings. In 1985, they opened a community service center and started a legal aid clinic, a family practice medical clinic, and a counseling service. They also continued a youth services program that included camps, tutoring, and after-school activities.

Faith-based partnerships are a powerful force for urban renewal when they unite the church and parachurch in a common cause.

The following year they added a shelter for homeless families and a volunteer housing program. Expansion continued in 1987 with the opening of a food and clothing pantry, an adult literacy program, and the expansion of Rock Church. The pace of growth has never slowed as new programs have been added, such as a prep school with over two hundred students. Along the way, Circle has raised and invested almost seven million dollars in capital and secured over twenty-two million dollars in real estate investment capital. They hold clear title to all their buildings and enjoy the full support of city government.

While Circle Urban and Rock Church provide leadership by example, untold numbers of volunteers have contributed the sweat equity that is making the future brighter for residents and their children. "When we moved to the corner of Central and Washington avenues in 1984," Glen recalls, "there were about fifty abandoned buildings in a two-block area. Most of those buildings have been restored or replaced. Circle Christian Development Corporation has restored about four hundred housing units and built eleven single-family homes."

These impressive programs and facilities are built on a solid foundation of cooperation, the cornerstone of which is a commitment to racial reconciliation. The value of reconciliation is something Glen knows about personally. A product of the all-white town of Ripon, Wisconsin, and an evangelical upbringing, he attended a conservative evangelical college. "In my studies," he says, "I began to see that the Bible had a lot to say about making the truth of the gospel visible. But for all my life I'd seen Christians separate the gospel into vertical and horizontal dimensions. The vertical dimension was the real gospel, getting saved and loving God. The horizontal dimension was the slippery slope to liberalism, the social gospel.

"This kind of thinking resulted in evangelicals sending missionaries thousands of miles away and spending millions to evangelize Africa while completely turning our backs on African-Americans in our cities. There was something wrong with that picture. So my wife and I did something about it: we moved into the inner city. That was more than thirty years ago and we've raised our kids here."

Having grown up in the white heartland and then spent his adult life in a predominantly black urban neighborhood, Glen has seen racism from both sides. "One of the long-term effects of racism has been segregated communities like the ones I've known. Most Americans live in neighborhoods of people like themselves, and work or go to school in homogenous environments. The church remains the most segregated of all institutions. Average white, middle-class evangelicals don't think about racism, except when it infringes on their lives. They generally don't have any African-American friends. They don't have any meaningful relationships with people who live in real poverty. In my extensive conversations with them, I've learned that most whites believe this country has leveled the playing field and solved the civil rights issues. However, when they get to know somebody of a different race, they begin to see the world through another's life experience, just like what happened to me."

"Reconciliation has a twofold reality," Glen wrote in the award-winning book *Breaking Down Walls: A Model of Reconciliation in an Age of Racial Strife.* "It has already happened, and yet it is still in process. We have been reconciled to God through conversion; we are a new creation. This is an accomplished fact. But this reconciliation must continue to work through us, crossing racial, social, and sexual barriers by means of the ministry of reconciliation empowered by God through Christ to work in and through us.

"The ministry of reconciliation can never be mere passive acceptance of a theological truth," Kehrein insists, "but must include active participation. Unfortunately, the Christian church at large— to state it in the most favorable way—is guilty of benign neglect. At best, we have been standing quietly on the sidelines while racism continues to wreck havoc on our society. Most Christians— white, black, Hispanic, and Asian—have not directly attacked the problems of racism."[2]

RACISM

Glen and Linc believe the racial divisions that have been with us since colonial times will be healed when Christians live out the truth of the gospel by loving our neighbors as ourselves. This involves following God where He leads. For the Kehreins and

Washingtons, it has meant swimming against the current of human-
ity fleeing the cities for the good life in the suburbs.

The Washington family moved to Chicago from Jacksonville,
Florida, where Linc had been a pastor. "When the Lord called us
to Chicago," he remembers, "we found ourselves in unfamiliar ter-
ritory. Many of the people we met didn't have good family struc-
tures. Most hadn't made it out of high school. In our area, which
is 99 percent African-American, there's about a 70 percent dropout
rate. These people were severely challenged on a variety of fronts.
I had evangelism strategies for reaching people, but I didn't see
them getting involved in the church. They might have an emotional experience, and after that we wouldn't see them again. It
took awhile for us to realize that if the church meant to help folks,
we had to meet their physical, as well as their spiritual, needs.

"One of the benefits of having this church-parachurch relationship," he continues, "is that it helps provide the resources necessary to meet physical needs. God has touched the hearts of folks
who have resources as well as those who have moved into our
area and have integrated. A number of doctors, lawyers, and other
professionals have accepted the missionary call to come. God is
using them to break down barriers."

Even as Pastor Washington affirms the value of what Circle
Urban Ministries brings to the equation of urban renewal, so Glen
Kehrein stresses the importance of the church.

> Through the Rock Church, they [our neighbors] find fam-
> ily—a loving, Christian family that faces its conflicts
> squarely and applies the healing power of the cross to
> each situation. In an increasingly secularized society we
> have consistently applied distinctly biblical solutions at the
> point of our community's need. Through financial part-
> nership with those who share our vision, we have been
> able to maintain our Christian distinctives while address-
> ing the physical needs that cry out all around us.[3]

Linc underscores that this is as it should be. "In the early church
there was economic development and equality. A number of

wealthier believers sold their possessions and shared with those in need. The bottom line for them was being in fellowship, as described in Acts 2: 'All the believers were together and had everything in common. Selling their possessions and goods, they gave to anyone as he had need. Every day they continued to meet together in the temple courts. They broke bread in their homes and ate together with glad and sincere hearts' (Acts 2:44-46)."

Jesus Christ designed His church to dispense salt and light. The preserving power of salt prevents decay. Light brightens even the darkest places. Because of this, Glen and Linc stress the critical role the church can have in urban reclamation. And the brave churches that successfully tackle the challenge often find a larger sphere of influence as a result. "For many years we have been able to share the ministry of reconciliation with others," Linc explains. "Not only are we a model for other churches in urban settings, but we are forcing the body of Christ at large to think about the mission field of the inner city."

RECONCILIATION

The hand-in-hand approach to urban renewal and racial reconciliation engenders credibility like nothing else. "I can be talking with someone in my neighborhood who says the white man is the problem," Linc says, "and I can point to my white partner in ministry and say Glen and his family live here. It's amazing how some of the walls come down after that."

"We call this incarnational love," Glen continues, "the same kind of love we experience from God through Jesus Christ. We know that God loves us because Jesus Christ came and walked among us. He demonstrated what love is all about. There's no substitute for that. The government can't pay people to show that kind of love."

Fortunately there are people willing to pay the price, such as Eleanor Josaitis, a suburban housewife, who started a civil rights organization called Focus:Hope in 1967. But instead of being admired for her social conscience, she was vilified by family and friends.

My husband, Donald, and I sold our home in the suburbs and moved into an integrated neighborhood in the heart of the city because I was not going to ask anybody to do anything I wasn't going to do myself. I'm still in the same house. My husband was very supportive, but it was not easy. My mother hired an attorney to take my five children away from me. My father-in-law disowned us. My brother-in-law asked me to use my maiden name so I wouldn't embarrass the family. There were difficult times; friendships were broken.[4]

"I don't believe we can experience our true divine identities," Pastor Linc says, "unless we are involved in cross-cultural relationships that are based on, and express, compassion. Life is enriched by giving, and giving is enhanced when it reaches beyond your comfort zone." Certainly the inner city is outside most people's comfort zone. "It's very difficult to do anything meaningful for the poor in the inner city without doing it cross-culturally," Kehrein points out.

Life is enriched by giving, and giving is enhanced when it reaches beyond your comfort zone.

"You have to go out of your way to find large pockets of poor white people. Not that they don't exist, but the ghettos in our cities are populated by minorities. Race and class have always been connected in America."

"If you asked the average African-Americans about racism," says Washington, "they would tell you it's alive and well in our cities. Of course the government has thrown a lot of money at the problem. They are trying to help folks in impoverished areas, and some of their programs are definitely meeting physical needs. But they can't address the deeper needs that are part of the problem. We're not looking to the government to fund our programs, although we do receive some monies because of what we're doing. The majority of the dollars that enable us to minister come from churches. This is as it should be since what we're doing is based on God's call on our lives. We recognize Him as our ultimate resource."

"The difference in a faith-based approach," says Kehrein, "is that while you start by feeding people and giving them a place to live, you realize these services by themselves bring little change. You have to also share a message of hope that will change people's hearts and get to the deep, systemic issues behind poverty. No amount of monetary assistance can address those deeper issues. I'm happy that the government is finally seeing the importance of faith-based initiatives and recognizing efforts like ours. We see the inner city differently from the way federal and state agencies do. We see the value of the people here because they're our neighbors. This is our home, and it's worth pouring our lives and resources into."

> *If you believe in something and have a passion for it, you have to stand up for it. And you have to be persistent, no matter how long it takes.*

Eleanor Josaitis says of her own three-and-a-half decades of working for racial reconciliation, "I discovered that three things are important to me: passion, persistence, and partnerships. I had a passion for civil rights, but I had to learn the art of persistence. If you believe in something and have a passion for it, you have to stand up for it. And you have to be persistent, no matter how long it takes. I also learned early on that you had better have partners."[5]

The passionate, persistent partnership between Circle Urban and Rock Church has fueled the dynamic transformation of their Austin neighborhood. Glen and Linc would like nothing more than to inspire others to follow their example. "But don't move ahead in ignorance," Glen says. "No one would throw on a rucksack, pack some Twinkies for lunch, and try to climb Mount Everest. He or she would prepare, look for an expert guide—acknowledge the need for help. Why should we think it takes less preparation to climb this mountain? Don't do it alone, and don't do it unprepared. Find like-minded people who are veterans in this area and ask: 'How can I work on reconciliation? How can I get involved?

How can I take the first step?'

"And then, don't just stand there—do something!"

Givers and Receivers
H. C. Warfield

I GREW UP BELIEVING there were two Gods, one for black people and one for white people. I mean this literally. I learned about the God of black people from my grandfather, who taught me that God is love. But the white folks in our town worshiped a different God, a God of hate. I would be forty-three years old before I realized there is only one God, and it is His children who didn't do right.

Even though Mississippi seethed with racial oppression in the 1950s and '60s, I hardly saw it as a child. Segregation was a way of life. At sixteen, I left home to join the Job Corps. For the first time in my life, I found myself outside Mississippi. I was treated like a human being. I hadn't recognized oppression until I experienced freedom. But it didn't last. I returned to Mississippi and got a job as a certified welder.

After a fight with some white men and a narrow escape from a lynch mob, I moved to Chicago. While the big city provided well-paying jobs, its racial climate was not much better. I learned that north or south, the white folks were all the same, and I hated every one of them. Alcohol provided my escape. Finally, crack cocaine removed my remaining dignity. Wasted by alcohol and drugs, I lost my children, my home, and my business. Life became a pitiful existence. I was a powder keg ready to explode. I carried hate in my heart and a gun in my pocket.

Hunger brought me to God. I had gone to churches all over Chicago for food, but not until I came to the food pantry of Circle Urban Ministries was I filled. While waiting for a bag of groceries, I heard the gospel. Circle Urban Ministries and Rock Church were holding revival meetings and I went because they served meals. Again I heard the gospel, and this time I responded. My heart was completely broken by God's love.

On top of that, a white guy from Hershey, Pennsylvania, stepped up and counseled me. God's love overcame my hatred as Bruce talked with me. That was the beginning of a new life. I realized there is only one God and that we are all His children. God also knew that to heal my heart, He needed to put me in a church committed to racial reconciliation. At Rock Church and Circle Urban Ministries I found black and white folks loving each other and serving God. But my relationship with Bruce is what made it all real.

Five years ago my hatred of white people totally consumed me. I felt justified because of what I had experienced. Today I can honestly say that God has taken away that hatred and given me love. It's a miracle.

FOR MORE INFORMATION, CONTACT
Circle Urban Ministries
118 North Central Avenue
Chicago, IL 60644
773-921-1446
www.circleurban.org

BOOKS THAT HAVE INFLUENCED GLEN KEHREIN AND LINC WASHINGTON
More Than Equals: Racial Healing for the Sake of the Gospel, Chris Rice and Spencer Perkins, Downers Grove, Ill.: InterVarsity Press, 2000.

My First White Friend: Confessions on Race, Love, and Forgiveness, Patricia Raybon, New York: Penguin Books, 1997.

Heart for the City: Effective Ministries to the Urban Community, John Fuder, ed., Chicago: Moody Press, 2000.

Restoring Communities at Risk: Doing It Together and Doing It Right, John Perkins, ed., Grand Rapids, Mich.: Baker, 1996.

Divided by Faith: Evangelical Religion and the Problem of Race in America, Michael Emerson and Christian Smith, New York: Oxford University Press, 2000.

Elayne Bennett is the founder and president of the Best Friends Foundation, a nonprofit organization she launched in 1987 while a faculty member of the Georgetown University Child Development Center. She holds a B.A. and M.Ed. in special education from the University of North Carolina, Chapel Hill. As a graduate student, she concentrated on resource and program development for special needs students and their families.

Elayne is the author of the Best Friends curriculum, which she also teaches in Washington, D.C. public schools. She is married to William Bennett, former Secretary of Education, and the best-selling author of several books. The Bennetts and their two children live in Chevy Chase, Maryland.

Chapter Four

A GIRL'S BEST FRIEND

Elayne Bennett and Best Friends Foundation

"Sex is the only form of human behavior viewed as uncontrollable in teenagers. If we taught them about driving the way we do about sex (how to speed and break laws without getting caught or paying the consequences), there would be more accidents and casualties among this age group than there are now."

Cal Thomas[1]

Social entrepreneurs are people who are touched by the needs in their community. Their minds and energies become engaged in finding ways to meet those needs. Their passion gives birth to practical programs that others can buy into. And as with any healthy offspring, the progeny looks a lot like its parent.

In the case of the Best Friends Foundation, it's easy to see the mother's heart and educator's concern of Elayne Bennett. Her contact with adolescent moms through her work at Georgetown University moved Elayne to start one of the most effective teen-help programs in the country at a time when young people need all the help they can get.

> *Social entrepreneurs are people who are touched by the needs in their community.... Their passion gives birth to practical programs that others can buy into.*

TEEN SCENE

The pathway to adulthood in America is littered with casualties. Over five million teens admit to binge drinking on occasion (downing five or more drinks at a sitting). Marijuana use among eighth graders increased more than 100 percent from 1991 to 1998. One in three high-school girls says she has thought about suicide at least once in a two-week period. The rate of increase in crimes committed by girls outpaces that of boys. America has the highest rate of sexually transmitted diseases in the developed world, with three million teenagers infected each year. The cost to our health-care system tops ten billion dollars a year and is escalating. The situation is even worse in our nation's capital, which posts a high school dropout rate of 44 percent and a high school pregnancy rate of 18 percent. The encouraging thing about this last statistic is that it represents an 8 percent drop from 26 percent as reported in the 1997 National Centers for Disease Control's Youth Risk Behavior Surveillance Survey.[2]

One cause of this dramatic decrease is the work of the Best Friends program. Girls in this innovative program have a pregnancy rate of *1 percent!* Best Friends is the brainchild of Elayne Bennett. In 1987, she worked as a faculty member of the Georgetown University Child Development Center doing research related to daycare. For the previous decade she had been working on program development for special needs students. One of the disturbing trends she noticed was the age at which girls were becoming mothers. "The mothers were getting younger and younger," Elayne recalls. "The seriousness of the problem finally hit me when we had a twelve-year-old mother. We were trying to educate one child on how to raise another. It made no sense. That is when I realized we should be putting our efforts into letting children have their childhood instead of having babies."

Why were these girls getting pregnant? Some of the instances resulted from sexual abuse, but Elayne discovered a predominant factor that Marian Howard had uncovered through her studies at Emory University. "When Marian asked a thousand mothers under sixteen the reason for their getting pregnant," Bennett quotes, "it was their inability to say no. And when she asked them what they would like to learn in a sex-ed class, over 85 percent said, 'how to say no without hurting my boyfriend's feelings.'"

Bennett started Best Friends later that year to teach girls how to say no to sex, drugs, and alcohol as a means of saying yes to life. "We do not particularly care whether our girls hurt their boyfriends' feelings," she says. "We empower them to realize that learning to say no is part of healthy human development, which leads to self-respect." As best-selling author Charles Swindoll says, "One of the marks of maturity is the ability to say 'no' without explanation."

In a *Reader's Digest* article written after Best Friends had been around for ten years, Mona Charen explains how it all began:

> One day [Elayne] and her husband [William, then Secretary of Education] talked through a plan to develop a network of girls, guided by older women, who support one another in the decision to postpone sex. Elayne took the idea to Phyllis Magrab, director of the Georgetown University Child Development Center, who instantly loved the idea. With Bennett sitting beside her, Magrab typed the first Best Friends program guide, a version of which is still distributed to every Best Friends girl today. Sexual abstinence and rejection of drugs formed the core of the program, but Bennett and Magrab aimed even higher. Best Friends would teach nothing less than how to live a happy, successful life.[3]

As Bennett told the NBC "Today Show" reporter, Jamie Gangel, in an interview in 2001, "The mission is to help young girls develop into young women of promise, young women with goals who are on their way to realizing their dreams, to help them not only mentally, but physically, emotionally, get to the point where they can be proud of themselves." Alma Powell, wife of Secretary of State Colin Powell and Best Friends' board member, also appeared on the program. "Every child needs the attention and the caring and the love of adults," Powell affirmed. "And they need to feel it not just at home, but be surrounded by it in other situations. And that's what this program does. It gives them a place to belong, and that's very important."

Message number one in the Best Friends' program is abstinence, which Bennett says has not exactly been at the forefront of our nation's educational efforts when it comes to sex. When Gangel asked, "How do you make abstinence cool?" Elayne replied, "By getting cool people who believe in it to help us."[4]

Bennett is adamant. "Our experience over the past fifteen years shows that girls want to hear the abstinence message and will respond positively when it is offered in a developmentally sound program in an educational setting that provides fun, companionship, and caring."

POSITIVE APPROACH

Best Friends is a long-term prevention program made available to girls as part of their school curriculum. Participants include a random selection of girls in the school per grade level, or in a smaller school, the entire class. With parental permission they start in fifth or sixth grade and continue through high school graduation. The curriculum provides at least 110 hours of in-school guidance and activities each year. The Best Friends Foundation, which licenses school systems to operate the program, publishes the curriculum, conducts educator training conferences, and provides technical assistance to schools. Currently there are about five thousand girls taking part in Best Friends Foundation program offerings in just over a hundred public schools in fourteen states, the District of Columbia, and the U.S. Virgin Islands.

In addition to the curriculum, program components include: role model presentations, weekly one-on-one mentor meetings, monthly group discussions, weekly fitness/dance, cultural activities, community service projects, and an annual end-of-year Family and School Recognition Ceremony. Of the mentoring component, Elayne says, "There is a mentoring craze right now, but people need to realize it is not as simple as pairing an adult with a child. Mentoring is great when used as part of a process. It cannot be the only part, though. There has to be a philosophy, a mission, a focus, and a curriculum. The core of our program is the Best Friends' curriculum, which has been carefully field tested, revised, and evaluated. It consists of seven units addressing friendship, love and dating, self-respect and decision-making, drugs, alcohol, STDs, and AIDS."

Having said this, the mentoring component is important in the Best Friends' approach. "The minimum requirement for our teacher-mentors is thirty minutes a week with each child. Our mentors reinforce the clear message of abstinence and provide a personal connection to our curriculum. These ladies are the heart of our program, offering the girls guidance while at school and a voice of reason to rely on," says Elayne.

"Women from the community [and now men for the Best Men program] are brought in as role models to discuss good decisions they have made and how those decisions have affected their lives. They stress the importance of healthy relationships, how they decided to get married, what marriage has meant to them, how they learned about true friendship and love, and what advice they have for their own children. Most importantly with role model speakers, our youth are exposed to community leaders, people who are determined to do their best and to be successful.

"Our group discussions," Bennett continues, "focus on concerns that all adolescent girls have. Our goal is to help them develop a sense of self-respect and self-worth through achievement and community service. We also want to help them make sound decisions and avoid at-risk behaviors, including sexual activity and substance abuse. We start with the topic of friendship because it is a key component in this equation for success in life. What these girls really need is not sex education but friendship. They are most concerned about their relationship with other girls. They want to know what friends do for each other. They want to know how to choose friends, how to identify someone who is not really a friend. We tell them a best friend is someone who helps make you a better person."

This holistic approach addressing issues most important to

youth, plus its impressive track record, has garnered Best Friends national attention. The National Campaign to Prevent Teen Pregnancy has honored the organization as one of the nation's most effective programs. Sarah Brown, director of the Campaign, says, "Best Friends is a wonderful contribution not only to reducing teen pregnancy, of course, but more generally to helping young girls grow into adulthood safely and with light in their eyes."[5]

While passion fuels much social activity, it is not enough. As an educator, Elayne has always believed that quality programs should conform to clear guidelines and produce positive results that are measurable and replicable. "Many efforts start with good intentions," she notes, "but are missing well thought-out curricula with a theoretical construct. Often they do not have clear-cut goals or ways of measuring whether they are truly successful. I tell people, do not put your time or money into programs that lack clear standards of behavior or methods of determining their effectiveness."

Do not put your time or money into programs that lack clear standards of behavior or methods of determining their effectiveness.

Don Fites, former CEO of Caterpillar, likes to say, "If you aren't keeping score, you're only practicing." Here's what the scorecard looks like for Best Friends, based on feedback from surveys given at the beginning and end of each school year. Dr. Stan Weed of the Institute for Research and Evaluation analyzed the findings from 2,631 girls collected nationally in the spring of 1999. Dr. Weed found:

- A sexual abuse reduction rate of 66 percent;
- A sexual intercourse discontinuation rate of 46.3 percent;
- A drug exposure reduction rate of 38 percent;
- A drug refusal rate of 81 percent;
- 75 percent said that they want to wait until marriage to have sex.

The 2000 survey found that Best Friends girls' behavior and attitudes were dramatically different from their peers:

- Less than 1 percent of Best Friends girls became pregnant during the year;
- Only 5 percent used illegal drugs;
- Only 4 percent had sexual intercourse;
- 92 percent said they want to wait until at least high school graduation to have sex.

In Washington D.C., where Best Friends began at Amidon Elementary School in 1987, 100 percent of the city's Best Friends' high schoolers have graduated from school, and sixty-three girls who entered the program by the seventh grade are attending college on scholarships provided by the Best Friends Foundation. In D.C. middle schools, 33 percent of eighth graders are sexually active, according to the Youth Risk Behavior Survey done by the Centers for Disease Control, while only 5 percent of Best Friends' girls from the same schools and communities are sexually active. And in seventh grade, the rate is 4 percent compared to 18 percent of their peers.

These impressive results are fueling Best Friends' nationwide expansion. After repeated appeals from several school systems, they began a Best Men program in 2000 with 150 middle school boys in the District of Columbia and Milwaukee. Three additional sites launched programs in 2001. The program provides boys with the tools and the environment needed to help them develop into responsible young men. The program is modeled after the Best Friends curriculum and includes many extracurricular activities that reinforce the Best Men messages of abstinence and respect.

Survey data collected during the 2001-02 school year shows that Best Men boys have significantly changed their behavior and attitudes toward sex, drugs, alcohol, and violence after one year of participating in the program. In the national program, 24 percent of the boys reported on the pre-survey that they had had sex prior to the beginning of the school year. Of that number, 40 percent reported on the post-survey that they had since stopped having sex. The data also demonstrates that 88 percent of the boys understand the difference between love and sex and 87 percent say they want to get married someday.

SOLID FOUNDATION

Although Best Friends functions as a program within the public schools, Bennett says there is a character development component that comes into play. "There are issues of character involved whenever you discuss subjects like commitment and marriage. There are moral reasons for abstinence from sex, drugs, and alcohol. We make it clear that these things are not good choices. One does not drink as a teenager; it is illegal. One does not take drugs, ever; they will hurt you and your family and destroy your dreams. And the best decision is to wait to have sex until you are married. One reason is that we believe all children deserve to begin life with two married parents."

Encouragement is the fuel of hope... people become what you encourage them to be, not what you nag them to be.

These guidelines may seem strict to some; however, the Best Friends' approach is not negative. It is not about nagging, but about encouragement. "Encouragement is the fuel of hope," insists motivational speaker and author Zig Ziglar. "It's true that people become what you encourage them to be, not what you nag them to be."

Best Friends provides adolescents with a youth development curriculum that is comprehensive and long-term. Girls and boys participate in positive, proactive group activities that help them acquire sound judgment, critical thinking, and life skills. "We have a lot of fun," Elayne says. "We have made the program cool and contemporary with our fitness and dance component. We even have our own theme song. Our high school girls participate in the Diamond Girls Jazz Choir and the Diamond Girls Jazz Dance Troupe. These performance groups are a part of the cultural enrichment and community service components required within the

Diamond Girls Leadership program. Our program is not about spending all your time saying no and sitting home by yourself. We show them the fun things they can do when they are young and how truly enriched life can be if they will avoid risk behaviors."

The tab for this program to date has been picked up by the private sector. Best Friends receives no federal, state, or local government assistance. "Our foundation funding comes from individuals, foundations, and corporate sources," Bennett explains, "although some of our replication sites are funded through Title V grant money. We have also applied for major federal grants. When it comes to government support, we hope our programs, which can document measurable results, will receive federal support to help them grow nationally. Currently, we are unable to serve many school systems who want our programs due to lack of federal funding."

More than the founder of a social service organization, Elayne Bennett is a mother whose own teens are facing the pressures addressed by her program. "I have an eighteen year old and a thirteen year old, so I am living with these issues every day. I believe each child has something positive to offer our society if given the opportunity to develop his or her potential. As adults, if we give our children our best, they will respond with their best.

"It is a lot of work," Elayne admits, "but the girls and boys make it worthwhile. They are wonderful."

Givers and Receivers

Cristina Evans-Duncan

AS I HAVE GROWN IN THE BEST FRIENDS PROGRAM, its meaning for me has evolved and changed just as my life has. When I entered the program in the eighth grade I was excited because I would get to meet more people, take field trips, and participate in the weekly jazz aerobics class. In retrospect, part of the reason why I liked Best Friends in junior high was that it was a single sex environment. It felt like when I went to Best Friends I was learning to be a young lady. I enjoyed having a place where I could concentrate on certain aspects of young womanhood that teachers and parents either don't know how to talk about, don't want to talk about, or can't find time to talk about. Now, as a young woman on the verge of graduating from high school, I am grateful for the messages Best Friends has instilled and the opportunities it has given me.

The themes that Best Friends focuses on—abstinence from sex, drugs, and alcohol—are clear and definite. Too often we get mixed messages about sex and drugs. Our peers and the media encourage us to try drugs at least once so that we can make an "informed decision" about whether or not to use them. At the same time, in our communities and in the news we constantly see the image of the strung-out junkie, warning us of what we could become. Decisions about sex are often more difficult. While our parents and church families tell it is morally wrong to engage in sex before marriage, phrases like "you're only young once," spoken by television, magazines, and advertising, promote a consequence-free environment that encourages sex without giving thought to pregnancy, disease, or emotional well-being.

Best Friends breaks away from the mixed messages and ambiguity by offering a clear message to teens: abstinence from dangerous behavior is the only way to ensure a happy, healthy, productive youth. The messages espoused by Best Friends gave me an alternative to the try-anything-once, no-responsibility attitude taken by most at my school. The alternative that Best Friends presented in many ways opened up doors for me and let me know that it was socially acceptable to not drink, smoke, or have sex. The main reason I felt so positively about the message of abstinence was that I saw other girls my age embracing it.

The Diamond Girls Program, as an extension of Best Friends, taught me more and more about the values and priorities central to young womanhood and adulthood. Through the March of Dimes and Make A Difference Day activities I learned the importance of community service and giving back to society. In my junior year I applied what I had learned and organized the participation of a group of Best Friends girls in the Washington, D.C. AIDS Walk. In college, I plan to study political science with an emphasis on public policy, and hope to eventually change lives for the better. Without Best Friends I probably would not have discovered my commitment to community service.

FOR MORE INFORMATION, CONTACT
Best Friends Foundation
4455 Connecticut Avenue, N.W.
Suite 310
Washington, DC 20008
202-237-8156
www.bestfriendsfoundation.org

BOOKS THAT HAVE INFLUENCED ELAYNE BENNETT
Restoring the Teenage Soul, Margaret J. Meeker, M.D., Traverse City, Mich.: McKinley & Mann, 1999.
Building a Healthy Culture: Strategies for an American Renaissance, Don Eberly, ed., Grand Rapids, Mich. and Cambridge, U.K.: Eerdmans, 2001.
The Educated Child: A Parent's Guide from Preschool through Eighth Grade, William J. Bennett, Chester E. Finn, Jr., John T. E. Cribb, Jr., New York: The Free Press, 1999.
Standing with Courage: Confronting Tough Decisions about Sex, Mary Louise Kurey, Huntington, Ind.: Our Sunday Visitor Publishing, 2001.

David Burdine recently retired as president of Bethesda Ministries and affiliated companies after thirty-three years of service, but continues to serve on the Bethesda Ministries and Mission of Mercy boards. He has served on the boards of several organizations and ministries, including Mission of Mercy, Every Home for Christ, the Assemblies of God Financial Services Group, the Equip Foundation, Meritcare, Inc., and KingdomBuy.com. He is also the former national chairman of Light-for-the-Lost.

In 1991, David was named the Alumnus of the Year by his alma mater, Evangel University in Springfield, Missouri, from which he holds a B.A. in business administration. In 1993 he received the Assemblies of God General Superintendent's Medal of Honor. In 2001, Northwest College conferred upon him an honorary doctorate. He and Sharon have been married since 1963. They have two adult children and five grandchildren and make their home in Colorado Springs, Colorado.

Chapter Five

MILLION DOLLAR DREAM: PROFITS FOR PHILANTHROPY

David Burdine and Bethesda Associates

*"It takes a lot of energy and
attention to give money away well."*

Bob Metcalfe[1]

David Burdine had a dream of giving away a million dollars in a single year before he retired. By the time he stepped down from the presidency of Bethesda Associates in June of 2002, the organization had already given over 95 million dollars to charitable, educational, and humanitarian efforts in more than a hundred countries. What started in 1959 with a few nursing homes in Nebraska became, under his leadership, a family of companies with assets in excess of 170 million dollars, including fourteen assisted-living facilities, land development and construction projects, Christian radio stations, office buildings, and storage facilities.

PLANTING SEEDS

Not your typical Type-A personality, Dave is the youngest of seven children. He was raised by a single mother, his father having left when he was five. Dave was so shy that he never went to youth camp and chose to live at home all four years of college. "My mother loved missionaries and had them in our home often," Dave recalls. "She constantly made sacrificial gifts to the church and missions. As a teenager, God put a burden in my own heart for the lost and less fortunate." But when Dave graduated from college in 1964, he didn't head overseas as a missionary. Instead, he followed the Lord's leading to Nebraska and became the first corporate controller of Bethesda Ministries. There were seeds to be planted for a future harvest beyond anything he could imagine.

Based in Ainsworth, Nebraska, population two thousand, Bethesda operated two nursing homes. Over the next several years the company grew, and in 1971, they sold three homes to put themselves solidly in the black. Shortly thereafter, Burdine felt God's leading to travel a different road. He moved to San Jose and became the controller of a commercial construction company. However, he never burned his bridges with Bethesda, and in 1976, when their president resigned, the board offered Dave the job. "It was anything but a plum position then," he says candidly. "Bethesda owned fifteen nursing homes and two acute-care hospitals, but they were in serious jeopardy of going bankrupt. Given their financial problems, the board wanted a president with a business background.

"When I went to San Jose I worked for a man named Phil Sondeno, a wonderful, generous Christian. He became a real mentor to me. I greatly respected his careful decision-making and his generous spirit toward the kingdom of God. My time with him gave me a different perspective on success. I learned how to use sound business practices to make money. My philosophy became one of maximizing profits and investing them wisely."

Not that there were any profits to work with when Dave returned to Nebraska. But in those darkest of times, he had a Damascus road experience to strengthen and sustain him. "It was a cold wintry night, no stars in the sky. A howling blizzard covered the road with ice as I drove home. I'd just had the most devastating disappointment in my career. The City Council of Lincoln had denied my request for a project that would have helped solve the wretched financial crisis we faced. I'd been president of Bethesda about four months. We were three million dollars in the red and had hundreds of thousands of dollars in past-due bills.

"I was desperate and sobbing to God, asking Him, 'Why?' Out

of the depth of my darkness I suddenly sensed a divine presence. God was in my car! And in the softness of His presence, I began singing,

Far away in the depths of my spirit tonight, lies a melody sweeter than psalm.

In celestial-like strains, it unceasingly falls, o'er my soul like an infinite calm.

Peace, Peace, Wonderful Peace, coming down from the Father above,

Sweep over my spirit forever I pray, in fathomless billows of love.[2]

"My tears stopped. My disappointment disappeared. My devastation evaporated. I had peace and I've had it ever since. Still, there was a lot of hard work ahead. One of my conditions for returning to Bethesda was that they would help me realize a life-goal of giving one million dollars in a single year to the kingdom of God before I retired. I was thirty-four then, and wanted to be financially able to retire by sixty. That meant I had twenty-six years. It turned out that after only a dozen years we gave away a million in 1988. That became a watershed year in another way. Our fiscal year ended in September and in October a company called Meritcare bought the thirty-four nursing homes we had in seven states. God ordained this sixty-million-dollar sale the very year we gave our first million.

"After clearing all debt," Burdine continues, "we ended up with about thirty-five million dollars in cash and other assets. We did the sale because we saw it as an opportunity to dream. Most of us on the board were at mid-life and we wanted the chance to use more of our time and energy for the kingdom. Our statement of purpose has always been 'To share God's love with the world.' It's the basis for everything we do in business and ministry. God had given us a passion for lost and hurting people. Now He blessed us with the financial ability to help thousands come to know His love.

INVESTMENT STRATEGY

With a solemn sense of stewardship, David and the rest of the board set about making the most of their seed money. They began investing in a variety of endeavors, including assisted-living facilities for the elderly. Over time they acquired or built 300,000 square feet of office space in Colorado Springs, where they relocated in 1979 because they felt it was a better place to raise their families. They also believed the city's growth presented some exciting business opportunities.

Bethesda's metamorphosis was well planned. "When we sold our nursing homes," Burdine explains, "we requested a private letter ruling from the IRS. This allowed us to establish four nonprofit companies and a proprietary company. The proprietary company would do the development and all the business functions not related to charitable activity. All the stock in the proprietary company is owned by one of the nonprofit companies. None of the board members has any personal ownership of the companies. Nor have we created any personal wealth out of the operation of Bethesda. Everybody works only for a salary and payment toward a pension plan. Six of the eight current members have more than twenty-six years of service with the organization."

The Bethesda board insists that while their obedience has been essential, it's not the reason for the ministry's success. Rather, it is God's delight in doing extraordinary things through ordinary people. Max Lucado notes this divine tendency in writing about the apostles.

> We need to remember that the disciples were common men given a compelling task. Before they were stained-glass saints in the windows of cathedrals, they were somebody's next-door neighbors trying to make a living and raise a family....But they were an ounce more committed than they were afraid and, as a result, did some extraordinary things.[3]

As president of the holding company, Dave's responsibilities included casting the vision and coordinating the efforts of the other board members. He set the organizational goals and planned future direction. He also supervised the contributions portfolios of Bethesda Ministries and Bethesda Associates. Given his long-standing passion for missions, why didn't Dave cash out after the sale and head overseas? There's no hesitation in his answer. "I felt I could be more effective using my business experience and my leadership skills to create the funds needed for ministry. Missionaries willingly sacrifice family, friends, and business opportunities to move abroad. However, they have to have partners who can provide them the resources they need to be effective.

"At Bethesda, we want maximum profit from our business operations in order to increase our ministry operations," says Dave. "We don't separate the two. How we make a profit and what we do with it are two sides of the same philanthropic coin."

> *Doing good should not be seen as a luxury affordable only after being earned, but rather as a way of life which integrates our values with our work.*

Many others have seen the symbiotic relationship between earning and giving, including Judy Wicks, owner of the White Dog Cafe in Philadelphia, who says, "Doing good should not be seen as a luxury affordable only after being earned, but rather as a way of life which integrates our values with our work....Doing well, or making a profit, should never be separated from doing good. Increasing profit while not increasing the well-being of mankind has led to most of society's major problems."[4]

Dave enjoys reminding people that giving isn't a one-way street. "It may be trite, but it's still true: you can't outgive God. He promises to cause our cup to overflow and that's been my life story. Ephesians 3:20 in *The Living Bible* says, 'Now glory be to God who by His mighty power at work within us is able to do far more than we could ever dare to ask or even dream of, infinitely, beyond our highest prayers, desires, thoughts or hopes.' I like this version because it includes *everything* that's ever been in our heads. When I wanted to give one million dollars in a single year, I never dreamed I would be part of a business operation that together with donors and friends would give ninety-five million dollars and counting!"

Burdine believes firmly in what he calls, "God's compound interest. The Lord takes your willingness to help people and compounds your ability to do so. Your effectiveness in helping others will be greatest along the lines of your talents, skills, and experiences. That's why businesspeople need to bring their skill-sets over to the non-profit sector. These skill-sets can help ministries organize themselves along sound business lines, which will make them far more effective. It will also give them more credibility with donors."

> *Your effectiveness in helping others will be strongest along the lines of your talents, skills, and experiences.*

There are costs associated with making such a move, however. "Businesspeople have to be willing to give up personal wealth and the building of estates for their heirs," Dave says. "But as one who has personally made the transition, I also have to add that I've lived a comfortable life. God has blessed me in my personal business investments. Matthew 6:33 has proven true for me: 'But seek first his kingdom and his righteousness, and all these things will be given to you as well.'"

Another facet of Bethesda's investment strategy is the premium it places on partnerships. "We use the word *partner* a lot because we aren't just check-writers," Burdine stresses. "To us, partnering means being involved with ministries on a monthly, if not weekly, basis. Every board member makes one or two trips a year overseas to investigate new opportunities. (Dave himself has visited more than fifty countries.) We also regularly reevaluate ministries we're involved with to make sure we want to continue working with them. As God's stewards, we're very results-oriented. We want to see a good return on our investments. This means getting as much information about a potential ministry partner as possible.

We want to know how they handle funds—how much goes to salaries, and how much to overhead, among other things."

Much of Bethesda's giving over the last several years has been channeled through Mission of Mercy. The ministry started in 1954 when Dr. and Mrs. Mark Buntain went to Calcutta, India. Dr. Buntain's death in 1989 raised serious concerns about the future of the work, which by then was feeding fifteen thousand women and children daily. They also provided medical care for hundreds of people and supported schools for thousands of students, the majority of whom were unbelievably poor.

Dave served on the Mission of Mercy board. He suggested to the Bethesda board that the two organizations merge and that Bethesda underwrite Mission of Mercy's administrative costs. That way the money coming from donors wouldn't have to go toward overhead and operating costs. The two boards enthusiastically agreed and the merger took place in 1990. Today, Mission of Mercy touches more than seventy-five thousand children in thirty of the world's poorest countries through its school and orphanage programs. Their help is freely given to all without regard to religion, social, or ethnic origin.

PASSION AND PEACE

Dave Burdine has a simple maxim for life: Passion is the key to success. "This is true in business, marriage, and life in general," he confidently asserts. "When Christ became my Savior, He infused me with a passion to fulfill both the Great Commission and the Great Commandment. I made a commitment in college—and when I married Sharon we affirmed the commitment together— to fling the net of God's love over as many lost and hurting souls as possible. We have never lost sight of that commitment we made almost forty years ago."

And yet, this fiery zeal hasn't created a frenetic pace at Bethesda. "God has given me a special gift of peace," Dave says. "It has enabled me to live a life free from worry and full of fun and fulfillment. This sense of peace has at times caused some of my associates to be concerned that I'm not taking life seriously enough.

I've had friends tell their bosses, 'You should have lunch with Dave because you're a workaholic and he can help you learn to slow down.' I've tried to lead by example and by structuring our corporate culture to discourage people from becoming workaholics. That's one reason we have a four-day workweek."

In his book *What They Still Don't Teach You at Harvard Business School,* Mark McCormack warns:

> Executives who treat their leisure time cavalierly or say they're too busy to take days off are fooling themselves. They don't appreciate the restorative powers of a long ski weekend or an afternoon squash game. They think of relaxation or free time as the time when nothing's going on. They tend to fill their free moments with trivialities. They trap themselves in a spiral of business that usually leads to disaster either in their personal life, or their business efficiency, or their health.[5]

This danger is even greater for those in the social sector who may be deceived into a false sense of immunity by the nobleness of their labors. People in ministry should be careful their zeal to serve God doesn't lead to burnout or moral failure.

People in ministry should be careful their zeal to serve God doesn't lead to burnout or moral failure.

"When I first came to Bethesda," Dave says, "I was very goal-oriented. But over time I became more concerned about who I was than what I did or even how much money we gave away. The moral and business failure of several church leaders had a tremendous impact on me. I moved from being so goal-oriented to being more concerned about my character and my relationships with God, my family, and others."

Not that Burdine has taken his responsibilities casually. He loves to quote the parable of the talents (see Matthew 25:14-30) in which the departing master entrusts his assets to his servants:

To one he gave five talents of money, to another two talents, and to another one talent, *each according to his ability.* [When the Master returned] the man who had received the five talents brought the other five. "Master," he said, "you entrusted me with five talents. See, I have gained five more." His master replied, "Well done, good and faithful servant! You have been faithful with a few things; I will put you in charge of many things. Come and share your master's happiness!" (emphasis added)

Dave and the rest of the folks at Bethesda are definitely Five Talent Types. And they certainly aren't waiting until heaven to share in their Master's happiness.

Givers and Receivers
Robert Solomon

I GREW UP IN CALCUTTA, a city of more than eighteen million people, and one of the poorest in the state of West Bengal, India. Slums comprise 80 percent of the city. The poverty is beyond imagination. There are 40,000 people per square mile, 1,000 people to a water faucet, 500 to a toilet.

My father, in his search for God, became a Hindu, a Muslim, and a Buddhist. Not finding answers in any of these, he became a Satan worshiper. Still, nothing satisfied his soul and he became an alcoholic, drinking away whatever money he could get his hands on. Mom would put my three sisters, a younger brother, and me to bed holding our stomachs and wondering when we would eat.

All of that changed one day because of a young missionary couple by the names of Mark and Huldah Buntain. They arrived in Calcutta on October 6, 1954. Mark constructed the first church to be built in Calcutta in a hundred years. Drunk and wandering the streets, my father heard music coming from the church. He stepped in and took a seat in the back. Before he left that evening he gave his heart to Jesus Christ. After that my entire family followed my father's footsteps and did the same.

Our family was then taken in and we kids placed in a school run by the organization the Buntains started called Mission of Mercy. They found sponsors for all five of us. If not for Mission of Mercy, none of us would have been educated. As a teenager I began to use the talent that God had given me in song. I entered talent contests and won many of them. I was offered contracts to sing in nightclubs for good sums of money. The offers were tempting, but God let me know that if I did not use my talent for Him, He would take it away.

A few years later God unexpectedly brought me the most precious thing in my life—my wife. She had come to Calcutta to help in the Mission of Mercy hospital as a nurse. We have been married for eighteen years now. After we got married we moved to the United States, something I never dreamed would happen to me. I went to work as an accountant for British Petroleum.

In 1996 I resigned from my job to spend full-time as a ministry representative for Mission of Mercy. Since then I travel and sing and share my story to bring hope to thousands of children who are just like I was. God, in His mysterious ways, has brought me from being a sponsored child to finding sponsors for needy children. I am honored that He would choose me, a poor child from Calcutta, to take His gospel to the end of the world.

I can't say enough about David Burdine and the others at Bethesda. I am privileged to partner with them in this great endeavor to extend God's kingdom. Had they not agreed to underwrite the administrative costs of Mission of Mercy after Dr. Buntain died, the doors to the schools, the hospital, and all the Mercy ministries would have been closed.

FOR MORE INFORMATION, CONTACT
Bethesda Associates/Mission of Mercy
15475 Gleneagle Drive
Colorado Springs, CO 80921
719-481-0100
www.missionofmercy.org

BOOKS THAT HAVE INFLUENCED DAVE BURDINE

The Greatest Miracle in the World, Og Mandino, New York: Bantam Books, 1983.

The Applause of Heaven, Max Lucado, Dallas: Word Books, 1990.

He Still Moves Stones, Max Lucado, Dallas: Word Books, 1993.

The Rhythm of Life, Richard Exley, Tulsa: Honor Books, 1987.

Destined for the Throne, Paul E. Billheimer, Minneapolis: Bethany House, 1996.

The Entrepreneur's Creed, Merrill Oster and Mike Hamel, Nashville: Broadman & Holman, 2001.

Jerry Wilger grew up in Albuquerque, where his dad owned a tire business. After dropping out of the University of New Mexico, he worked for his dad for a time and then became an aircraft salesman. Before age thirty, he was twice named Beechcraft Salesman of the Year.

In 1972 Jerry took over the family business and started other entrepreneurial ventures. He sold his businesses in 1994 to get reacquainted with his family and to work on lowering his golf score. That was before becoming the national director of Prison Fellowship's InnerChange Freedom Initiative. Jerry and his wife, Glenna, have been married more than forty years and have two married children. They divide their time between Scottsdale, Arizona, and Durango, Colorado.

Chapter Six

SET FREE, STAY FREE: PRISON REFORM THAT WORKS

Jerry Wilger and Prison Fellowship's InnerChange Freedom Initiative

"Master, what are you talking about? When did we ever see you hungry and feed you, thirsty and give you a drink? And when did we ever see you sick or in prison and come to you?" Then the King will say, "I'm telling the solemn truth: Whenever you did one of these things to someone overlooked or ignored, that was me—you did it to me."

Matthew 25:37-40 (MSG)

The United States already has the highest incarceration rate in the world," says former drug czar William Bennett, "with more than two million persons in federal and state prisons and local jails (in 1980, the figure was just over five hundred thousand). Today we deploy almost three-quarters of a million full-time, sworn law enforcement officers, and Americans spend more than fifteen billion dollars annually on personal security systems."[1]

The main architectural feature of the modern American prison is a revolving door. Two out of three released prisoners are re-arrested within three years. But a new incarceration model called InnerChange Freedom Initiative (IFI) hopes to change all that. At the request of the State of Texas, Prison Fellowship launched a 24/7 Christian prison program at the Carol Vance Unit near Houston. The program served more than a hundred inmates by the end of its first year, and two hundred inmates by the end of its second. Modeled after a successful program in Sao Paolo, Brazil, the IFI program begins eighteen to twenty-four months before an inmate's release and includes six to twelve months of post-release aftercare.

"This twenty-four hour 'Christian prison' gives offenders a chance to turn their lives around," says IFI director Jerry Wilger. "Inmates volunteer for the program and must meet several criteria before being accepted. We introduce them to Jesus Christ and teach them how to live for Him. We create a loving environment— albeit in prison—with caring staff and quality curriculum, but the power to change lives comes from God. The religious angle causes problems for some; however, as the results are becoming evident, even the skeptics can't deny that what we're doing works better than anything else."

FLYING HIGH

This innovative program has an innovative director. Jerry Wilger's entrepreneurial bent has been influenced and encouraged by his father's powerful example. "Dad taught me and my brother that there is no free lunch," he recalls. "We grew up believing we could do anything we set our minds to. Dad proved this in his own life, and his success afforded us a comfortable lifestyle. What became clear to me growing up was that work came first, personal pleasure second, and marriage and family third. God didn't even make the list.

"I dropped out of college when I was twenty, married Glenna a year later, and worked for my dad until I was twenty-four. Leaving my dad's business to go to work for the Texas Beechcraft distributor as an aircraft salesman caused a rift between him and me, but it was probably the single most significant factor in my later business success. When I left Albuquerque, Dad expressed doubts that I'd ever succeed at anything. However by the time I turned thirty, I'd been named Beechcraft Salesman of the Year two years in a row.

"My success in an extremely competitive market gave me confidence in my ability to compete. And my experiences in selling personal and corporate aircraft to highly successful businessmen gave me the self-assurance I would need later to move beyond my comfort zone to start new businesses or take over others that were failing."

Eventually his dad acknowledged Jerry's success, and in 1972 Jerry returned to take over, with his brother, the family tire business. "I merged it with a Denver-based company in 1977," Wilger says, "and sold out in 1982 when my new faith in Christ began to put a strain on my relationship with my business partner. Forty-three years old is too young to retire, but I was worn out and needed a rest. I spent the next two years flying gliders and getting acquainted with my children. At least, that's what I thought I was doing. But God had something else in mind."

God certainly wasn't in the foreground in Jerry's early years. "I grew up in a Catholic environment," he says, "including parochial school. But when I got older, I became disenchanted with Catholicism and anything religious. However, after my mom died, it became apparent to me that there had to be something more to this 'God thing' than I had experienced growing up. I started to look at what the Bible said about a relationship with God. My wife, who had recently accepted Christ, had a lot of friends praying for me. Their prayers, and the words of my friend, Dave Cauwels, were instrumental in my coming to know the Lord."

PRISON REFORM

While Jerry enjoyed his freedom, God had prison in mind for his future. "I didn't know what I wanted to do next," he recalls. "Then Dave Cauwels, an executive board member of Prison Fellowship, asked me to conduct pre-release seminars on how to apply for, and keep, a job. The experience opened my eyes to the appalling lack of preparation given inmates to face life on the outside. At one point I called the New Mexico Secretary of Corrections to tell him what a lousy job the corrections system was doing. Instead of getting angry, he enlisted my help in setting up a prison industries program to give inmates job training while still incarcerated."

Wilger's involvement escalated quickly. During the next two years he served as a volunteer administrative assistant to the

Secretary of Corrections. He worked in every part of the prison system, looking for ways to save money, improve effectiveness, and promote rehabilitation. His efforts to change the system eventually attracted the attention of the governor of New Mexico, who fired him from his unpaid position.

"My career in corrections ended when the governor asked me to resign," Wilger says with a chuckle. "His explanation for firing me was that, 'People in our state don't want the government to be run like a business.'"

After the challenges of trying to make the corrections system work, retirement seemed boring to Jerry. So he got back into business. "Air ambulance services were in their infancy in the '80s," he says. "I designed and implemented a service for hospitals in New Mexico. Another aviation opportunity presented itself in Santa Fe and I took on the challenge, moved there, and ran both businesses at the same time."

In 1993 the Wilgers moved to Scottsdale, Arizona, where Jerry managed his businesses long-distance. In 1995, when buyers came along who wanted those companies more than he did, Jerry sold them and concentrated on becoming a zero-handicap golfer. Life on the links was great for Jerry, and then God played the Corrections Card again. On a visit to his friend Dave, he met with Chuck Colson, the founder of Prison Fellowship. This former aide to President Nixon started Prison Fellowship in 1976 after his own stint in prison on a Watergate-related charge. By 1999 they were operating over fifty field offices with more than forty-six thousand volunteers and three hundred and fifty paid staff nationwide. Today the nonprofit Christian organization serves prisoners in correctional facilities across the country and around the world.

As Jerry remembers it, "Chuck mentioned an opportunity Prison Fellowship had to start a full-time Christian rehabilitation program in Texas. Recalling my involvement with the Corrections Department in New Mexico, he asked if I'd serve on the advisory board. I agreed. We launched the program and eighteen months later Chuck asked me to become the director. He figured my business experience and corrections knowledge might give the fledgling program the focus it needed. The only reason I could come up with for saying 'no' was that my golf handicap would suffer. That seemed like a pretty lousy excuse to give God. So, at age fifty-eight, I began the greatest adventure of my life."

As the director of IFI, Wilger negotiates with state officials and oversees staff training and program implementation in several states. "The goal is to take the program national," he says. "Many states have asked us to start programs, but we want more time to substantiate our recidivism numbers. Recidivism is figured on a two- to three-year period after someone is released from prison. The various Departments of Corrections are saying if we could reduce recidivism 10 to 15 percent, it would be the biggest bell ringer in fifty years. We think we can reduce recidivism 50 percent or more. But even if we reduce it by a conservative 15 percent in Texas, for every dollar the state puts into the program, they will get back $3.18 in savings."

In praise of their efforts in the Lone Star State, then-governor George W. Bush said, "The collective wisdom is that if the State of Texas, through a program like InnerChange, can change a person's heart, we have a very good chance of meeting state objectives like reducing recidivism. InnerChange is exciting because it does more than preach the gospel—it encourages people to stay involved with prisoners, changing one life at a time."[2]

Anchored in biblical teaching, education, and Christian camaraderie, the IFI program has three phases. Phase One focuses on the prisoner's internal healing process and seeks to rebuild spiritual and moral filters. Phase Two puts inmates in real-life settings and prepares them for life after prison. Inmates spend much of the day in off-site work programs, returning in the evenings for classes. Phase Three helps the inmate to assimilate back into the community through productive relationships with family, the church, and the workplace.

To Wilger, one of the most exciting aspects of IFI is the willingness of others to become personally involved. "We find many successful businesspeople coming in as volunteers, including presidents of companies and CEOs. They are mentoring convicts and equipping them to make it on the outside. This is a motivating factor for many inmates who think, 'If this guy is so important and he's willing to spend time with me, there's got to be something to this Christian deal.'"

Reporting in *USA Today*, William Mattox Jr. says,

This remarkable program is quite different from traditional conservative approaches to criminal justice ("lock 'em up and throw away the keys"). It's also different from conventional liberal approaches ("social problems like poverty and racism are largely responsible for criminal behavior"). Nevertheless, (former inmate) James Peterson believes there is an even better term than compassionate conservatism for what InnerChange offers. "If you ask me," he says, "I'd just call it real Christianity."[3]

The Bible calls it a reason for eternal reward in Matthew 25, where Jesus commends those who visited Him while in prison in the guise of "the least of these brothers of mine" (see 25:34-40).

CROSSING OVER

Social entrepreneurs face many adjustments in crossing over from business to the social sector, and Jerry has been no exception. He has a few pieces of practical advice to those making the transition. "Don't sell yourself short if you go to work for a nonprofit. When I moved from the non-paying advisory board to the national director position, I asked for a salary—for three reasons: First, it wasn't feasible for me to put my full time and effort into the project without some compensation. But, more importantly, I felt that if they didn't like my performance, they might not get rid of me because I was free and someone else would cost them. I also know that people believe they get what they pay for. If they don't pay for something, or someone, they tend not to value it."

While the program Jerry directed was new, it grew out of an existing ministry with established ways of doing things. "Trying to change operating procedures as I identified problems sometimes damaged my relationships with coworkers," he admits. "Such conflicts are inevitable, but their severity can be lessened by taking a simple precaution. When assuming a leadership role—especially in a nonprofit context—make sure your tasks and the authority to accomplish them are clearly defined up front."

This is as essential for leaders as for those who are responsible for producing results. "One of my strengths is my goal orientation," says Wilger. "I require my staff to work toward specific goals within a given period. I don't let things roll on and on. This results orientation isn't the norm in most ministry settings, and I'm challenged on this a lot. Someone will say, 'Jerry is too hard on people,' or, 'He's too demanding.' But if I learned anything from my selling career and management experience, it's that time is money. Using time wisely is as central to success as keeping an accurate balance sheet and making sure the bottom line can be printed in black. Like government, most ministries have a more relaxed view of time than what's found in the private sector. I agree that the timing of God's work is in God's hands. But I also believe we're accountable for accomplishing the tasks God gives us in a timely manner. It's hard to keep things moving in an organization that's more inclined to *meet and talk* than to *do*.

When assuming a leadership role—especially in a nonprofit context— make sure your tasks and the authority to accomplish them are clearly defined up front.

"Another roadblock to efficiency I've encountered is what I've dubbed the 'ministry view' of employees. Because of a ministry's compassion for people—which is good— unproductive employees are seldom terminated—which is bad. Either they are left in place and their jobs don't get done, or they are moved to other positions. The danger of the latter is that it simply changes, and sometimes expands, the person's sphere of ineffectiveness."

Negotiating is a key part of what leaders must do both inside and outside of their organizations. Jerry feels particularly adept at it. "Being able to see both sides of an issue gives me the ability to put myself in both sets of shoes and makes it easier to negotiate a win-win solution. I always try to make deals on terms that will benefit both parties. I've also learned that no one is unapproachable. Whether the CEO of a Fortune 500 company, or a senator, or a governor, I feel comfortable negotiating with anyone God brings into the picture."

On the personal level, Wilger warns against the danger of isolation. "Social entrepreneurs need the spiritual input and honest feedback of a few close friends. I am vitally connected to a couple of strong, Bible-teaching churches. I spend time with the senior pastors of both. They are my friends. We share openly with one another, play golf, and have dinner together. When I'm out of town I feel the drain of not having their input."

Social entrepreneurs need the spiritual input and honest feedback of a few close friends.

In his book *Wild at Heart,* John Eldredge stresses how important it is for men (and women) to have relationships that go deeper than mere accountability groups.

> Thanks to the men's movement the church understands now that a man needs other men, but what we've offered is another two-dimensional solution: "Accountability" groups or partners. Ugh. That sounds so old covenant: "You're really a fool and you're just waiting to rush into sin, so we'd better post a guard by you to keep you in line."

> We don't need accountability groups; we need fellow warriors, someone to fight alongside, someone to watch our back. . .we need men to whom we can bare our souls. But it isn't going to happen with a group of guys you don't trust, who really aren't willing to go to battle with you. It's a longstanding truth that there is never a more devoted group of men than those who have fought alongside one another, the men of your squadron, the guys in your foxhole. It will never be a large group, but we don't need a

large group. We need a band of brothers willing to "shed their blood" with us.[4]

Next, there's the issue of personal holiness. "We have got to be sure that our lives are as sin free as we can make them," Jerry says. "As humans, we are going to sin; we know that. But if we have sin in our lives that we aren't willing to get rid of, then we have greatly diminished the ability of the Spirit to work in us. Effectiveness in serving others only comes from reliance on, and closeness to, the Holy Spirit."

Jerry illustrates his final caution to SEs with an outstretched hand. "Hold your involvement with an open hand. The God who gives you a specific task can also take it away. Don't ever think the work is yours—it's His. And He knows how best to use His people."

A profound sense of gratitude underlies everything Wilger does. It motivates him—a man who has climbed to the top of the success ladder—to care about those who don't even know where to find the first rung. "Jesus Christ died for my sins and has given me the gift of eternal life," he says fervently. "I owe Him everything. When I think back on how He has prepared me for this venture, there's no way I could say no to His plan. God has given me a heart for inmates. The joy of seeing someone who is down in the gutter come to know Christ and be changed from the inside out, that's better than a seven-digit bank account!"

Hold your involvement with an open hand. The God who gives you a specific task can also take it away.

Is it better than a zero handicap?

Jerry laughs. "I don't think anyone cares about my golf handicap, not even me anymore. I get more pleasure out of what IFI is accomplishing than anything I've ever done in my life."

Givers and Receivers
James Peterson

James Peterson spends his days helping newly released prisoners adjust to freedom. He listens to stories about job searches. He prays with a former inmate whose wife is sick, and he counsels another who's looking for an apartment.

Mr. Peterson knows what the men are going through. The forty year old served three years and four months in prison for embezzling 60,000 dollars from the Houston-area trucking company where he worked.

Texas Governor George W. Bush spoke admiringly of Mr. Peterson during campaign speeches. Chuck Colson's Prison Fellowship Ministries made a video about him. That's because James Peterson did something few other Texas prisoners have done: He turned down parole so he could complete an eighteen-month experimental Christian counseling program. Mr. Peterson believes so strongly in the InnerChange Freedom Initiative that he now works for it.

"This was an opportunity to finish a task," explains Mr. Peterson, who spent an extra ten months behind bars. "I needed to make a commitment."

The former inmate says the voluntary, faith-based program changed his life through Bible studies, counseling sessions, and Scripture-based classes in life skills. He was only nine months into it when he learned that he would be paroled in April 1998. That's when the former bookkeeper started thinking about staying behind bars.

InnerChange officials at first didn't think he was serious.

"I wanted to make sure James was doing this for the right reasons," says Jack Cowley, InnerChange's national operations director. "I wanted to make sure it was something God wanted him to do."

Mr. Peterson says it was a gut-wrenching choice. His seven-year-old daughter, Lucy, lives less than three miles from the prison, yet the former inmate had seen her only twice because she was afraid to visit. Mr. Peterson's hazel eyes fill with tears as he describes the days he spent praying about whether to turn down parole or leave prison so he could see his daughter.

Mr. Peterson stayed. He also wrote to all of his former employers to apologize for stealing money. One of them, nursing home administrator Wesley Stevens, says he hesitated but then wrote back. The two met three times before he believed that Mr. Peterson had really repented. Mr. Stevens, a Houston minister, led a reconciliation service that was filmed for a Prison Fellowship video. He and Mr. Peterson still correspond.

Mr. Peterson has received a lot of praise since he started working for InnerChange, but he says he carries Mr. Stevens' words in his heart: You have become the man I thought you were the day I hired you.

Says Mr. Peterson: "I have finally learned to be at peace with myself and what I have done."[5]

FOR MORE INFORMATION, CONTACT
InnerChange Freedom Initiative
Prison Fellowship Ministries
1856 Old Reston Avenue
Reston, VA 22180
703-478-0100
www.prisonfellowship.org

BOOKS THAT HAVE INFLUENCED JERRY WILGER
Born Again (20th anniversary ed.), Charles W. Colson, Old Tappan, N.J.: Fleming H. Revell, 1996.

Loving God, Charles W. Colson, Grand Rapids, Mich.: Zondervan, 1997.

The Heart of the Problem: How to Stop Coping and Find the Cure for Your Struggle, Henry R. Brandt, Kerry L. Skinner, Nashville: Broadman & Holman, 1997.

Experiencing God: How to Live the Full Adventure of Knowing and Doing the Will of God, Henry T. Blackaby, Nashville: Broadman & Holman, 1998.

Duncan Campbell has more than thirty years of timberland investment and forest industry experience. He is a CPA and attorney, holding a B.S. in business administration and a doctor of jurisprudence degree from the University of Oregon. In 1981 he founded The Campbell Group, a successful timber investment business in Portland, Oregon. By 1986, assets under management totaled 4.5 million dollars, and by 2001 they had grown to 1.7 billion dollars.

United Asset Management Corporation (UAM) acquired the stock of The Campbell Group in 1989; however, Campbell and the other principal officers still handle the direction and daily operations of the group. Duncan has worked on the Governor's Children Agenda in Oregon, and is a past chairman of the Multnomah County Juvenile Services Commission. He has three children and has been married to Cindy since 1976.

Chapter Seven

INVESTING IN
GENERATION NEXT

Duncan Campbell and Friends of the Children

"Many social entrepreneurs have been successful in the first half of their lives in some business or professional enterprise. They have now become the founders of social entrepreneurial enterprises and perhaps hired executive directors and staffs to execute the programs. What I've frequently found is that these social entrepreneurs are very attuned personally to the constituency they are serving."

Bob Buford[1]

Duncan Campbell believes that a loving relationship with a positive adult role model can save a child's life. The product of a tough North Portland neighborhood and a dysfunctional family, Duncan yearns to give society's most at-risk kids what he and his brother wanted most growing up—a caring adult friend.

Duncan's alcoholic parents provided little support and lots of shame for him as a child. "I never had a sense of hope, other than I wanted to be different from my parents," Campbell says. "And I wanted it so badly that it encouraged me." It "encouraged" Duncan through college, into business, and on to a second-half career as a social entrepreneur. In 1993 he started Friends of the Children with almost two million dollars from the sale of his timber investment firm. Nowadays he divides his time between running the business for the current owners and promoting Friends of the Children.

DEDICATED MENTORS

Friends of the Children operates on the firm assumption that kids can be successful in life if given the encouragement of adult friendship. Experts agree on how essential a caring adult is to the healthy development of a child. What is unique about Friends' work with at-risk kids is how they ensure the stability of a mentoring relationship by paying for it.

The "Friends" in Friends of the Children are full-time employees who spend a minimum of four hours a week with up to eight children, no more. They work with their kids on a wide range of life skills, including problem solving, conflict resolution, and the importance of honesty, respect, and hard work. They provide tutoring and model sound values, which the child has likely not seen up close. Perhaps most important, they just hang out together.

As advocates for their kids, the Friends often act as the key link to a child's total environment, including family, school, and community. On the child's behalf they may tap into resources such as family counseling services and health care. But they aren't meant to be substitute parents. They don't give money to their child's family or help family members deal with state agencies.

The "children" in Friends of the Children are the most vulnerable kids, those who are in danger of school failure, substance abuse, gang involvement, teenage pregnancy, and criminal behavior. "We work with the most difficult children in the most difficult schools in the community," says Campbell, "not the most athletic, brightest, or prettiest. We're committed to loving them, caring for them, and nurturing them when everybody else has written them off. We select kids in the first grade for the program with input from people in the community. And once in, we promise to stick with a child until he or she finishes high school. We start with first-graders because they are still impressionable to values and still have a sense of hope, despite their difficult circumstances. The earlier we begin, the stronger the impact."

Parents must approve of their child being in the program. "We don't say to a parent, 'Your child's one of the most difficult kids in school; we're going to help her,'" explains Duncan. "Rather, we say, 'Your child has the opportunity to have a relationship that will encourage and support him through his school years.'"

The epoxy that holds "Friends" and "Children" together is a two-part mix of planning and accountability. Duncan is no mere sentimentalist with a soft spot for kids; he is a shrewd investor who expects a return on his investment. Before launching Friends, he did extensive research to find out what really worked with children in dysfunctional situations. When he confirmed that long-term mentoring produced the best results, he hit upon what would become the distinctive of his approach.

> *Good planning is crucial; without it you won't get where you want to go unless you're incredibly gifted or uniquely blessed.*

With a clear goal in mind and a proven way to reach it, Campbell put together a plan. "I believe strongly in planning," he insists. "That includes a strategic plan, a medium-term plan, and an annual plan. Good planning is crucial; without it you won't get where you want to go unless you're incredibly gifted or uniquely blessed. And people need to be held accountable to the plan. That's why I'm big on benchmarks and outcomes.

"It's also important," Duncan continues, "to make sure those executing the plan are mature in character and have the competence to make it work. Many people want to do something, but they lack the capacity to be successful. This is why our most critical decision is the selection of Friends. Our hiring process is very sophisticated. We do extensive criminal and background checks on candidates. They fill out a questionnaire and go through a series of interviews. If they check out to this point, we have them spend time with an existing Friend and a Child. We try to assess if they have what we call the gift of relationship. Finally, there's a formal interview with me and three or four others."

The average Friend is twenty-six years old. Most have a college degree and some experience working with children. Half are men, half are women. Fifty percent are African-American, 30 percent are white, 10 percent are Latino, and 10 percent are of mixed race. These numbers almost match the ethnicity of the children, which is 43 percent African-American, 47 percent white, 5 percent Latino, and 5 percent of mixed race.

Campbell wants his Friends to consider what they do a career, and most Friends who began with the program are still in it. He offers 401(k) benefits, insurance, and a modest monthly expense account. Wouldn't it be cheaper to use volunteers? "The problem with volunteers," says Campbell, "is that most of them quit when the novelty wears off. Friends are hired at salaries comparable to what first-year teachers earn to enable them to make a career of mentoring. Mentors need to have persistence. It is the most critical element in what we do, other than faith."

This long-term, full-time approach to mentoring reflects the actual meaning of the word, as Gregg Levoy notes. "The term 'mentor' comes from a character in *The Odyssey* by the same name. He was an old man who was entrusted by Ulysses with the care and education of his son, Telemachus, while Ulysses was away at the Trojan War, a job that ran into quite a bit of overtime, as Ulysses finished up with the war but was then blown around the Aegean for the next ten years."[2] Interestingly, that's about the same amount of time Friends spend with their kids.

Others have verified the effectiveness of the program. "What makes them (Friends) so good is that they have the ability to forge a one-on-one relationship with a child and make a difference in the lives of kids who have come from demolished backgrounds," says Betty Uchytil, assistant administrator for field operations of Oregon's Office of Services to Children and Families. "One person, over time, can turn a life around. It is not something state agencies can do."[3]

DYNAMIC EXPANSION
Friends of the Children has preformed well since its inception and has grown from three mentors working with twenty-four children in 1993 to thirty-four Friends serving over 260 kids in the Portland area in 2002. The program started in a single school, but now has

kids in almost ninety elementary schools. Chapters have also been started in Chester, Pennsylvania; Cincinnati, Ohio; Washington, D.C.; Seattle, Washington; and Klamath Falls, Oregon, with plans to launch at least four new programs annually, including openings in New York City, San Francisco, and Wilmington, Delaware. By the start of 2002, the program was serving nearly six hundred children in eleven cities.

The expansion is being driven by the best advertising in the world. "All of these programs have started due to word of mouth," Duncan reports. "Somebody told somebody else that they needed to meet us. Three ex-Microsoft people are initially funding the Seattle work. Steve Young, the ex-quarterback for the 49ers, is funding the San Francisco effort. Foster Friess of Brandywine Funds has been instrumental in getting the chapters started in Chester and Wilmington. The national office in Portland sets the standards and trains the executive directors and the Friends themselves. From here we monitor the programs and maintain quality standards, but the programs themselves have to be driven and funded by the local communities."

Two reasons why Friends of the Children has been able to expand rapidly are its flat structure and the low overhead of the head office. They maintain a lean administrative staff, just six people, which allows for over 85 percent of the funds they raise to go directly into kids' lives through underwriting the salaries of Friends. However, the most powerful growth factor continues to be their success, which has been well documented.

> Northwest Regional Educational Laboratory (NWREL) in Portland, a nonprofit organization financed by the U.S. Department of Education, has launched a ten-year study of the program. In addition to monthly reports from Friends, the laboratory receives assessments filled out by teachers, school principals, parents, and the children themselves. Interim reports show that few of the children have had contact with the criminal justice system. Nearly all of them avoid drugs and alcohol.[4]

"Not only are these kids avoiding trouble with the law," Campbell asserts, "they have shown marked improvement in school attendance, grades, standardized test scores, teacher evaluations, behavior, social adjustment, and personal hygiene. The NWREL reports document consistent progress in that our kids are staying in school, they have better relationships with peers and family, and their self-esteem and hopes for the future have improved. Almost all of the children are involved in summer camps and after-school activities that keep them doing positive things."

"Such success does not come cheap," writes Margery Stein in *Parade* magazine. "Each child costs the program $5,000 a year. 'But you're preventing costly intervention later,' said Gary Walker of Public-Private Ventures, a social-research organization in Philadelphia. 'A year in prison can cost more than five times as much.'"[5]

In another interview, Walker goes further, "In my professional life, I've seen only a few programs that I think have a shot at really making a difference. I don't casually toss words around like 'brilliant' and 'unique,' but what Campbell did is brilliant and unique. What he created in Portland could change the way this country tries to help its children."[6]

DUNCAN'S LEGACY

"Three things went into starting Friends of the Children," elaborates Duncan. "First, I was one of these children as a youngster. Second, in my early twenties I worked at the juvenile court as a child-care worker. I saw kids come through that I knew wouldn't be there if they'd had a relationship with a caring adult. Third, near the time I came to Christ, I sold my business, which created financial resources.

"I actually looked to the church when I was young," he recounts. "I went to a Baptist church and even became president of the Baptist youth fellowship in grade school. I looked for Jesus, but never felt like I found Him. When I got into my late teens and early twenties, I became an atheist. But in my thirties, I was no longer foolish enough to think that God didn't exist. Then about ten years ago, someone invited me to Bible Study Fellowship. At that same time someone else invited me to church. The Holy Spirit began touching me. All the barriers I had against God crumbled and I committed my life to Jesus Christ as the one, true Son of God."

At first, Duncan says he was angry with God for not touching him earlier in life. However, he soon came to peace about his own past and was determined to change the future for children like himself. Campbell says it this way, "Before I died, I wanted to change one child's life in reality. And I knew that the most powerful way to change lives is through committed, long-term relationships. If Jesus was here in the flesh, He would build relationships with children and love them the way a Friend does. He's the one who said, 'Let the little children

The most powerful way to change lives is through committed, long-term relationships.

come to me, and do not hinder them, for the kingdom of heaven belongs to such as these' (Matthew 19:14). As His followers we should be reaching out into our communities and caring for children who made no choice to be in difficult circumstances. A seven year old has no choice about where he or she is."

Since faith is such a paramount motivation for Duncan, why didn't he make Friends of the Children an overtly Christian ministry? His answer: "I struggled for a couple of years with whether to make Friends what's known as a 'first-tier ministry.' First-tier ministries are groups like Youth for Christ or Young Life. Their primary purpose is evangelism. A 'second-tier ministry,' on the other hand, reflects the love of Christ through actions and not so much through what's said. A second-tier ministry can often reach a broader world, which is why I decided to go with this approach."

Campbell has been very successful in business and can afford to be a social entrepreneur. "All my resources belong to God," he gratefully acknowledges. "I have to be a good steward and do what I believe He has called me to do. What wealth has done is give me the opportunity to create Friends on a wider scale. And while our family was the catalyst at the start, almost all the funding today comes from individuals, businesses, fund-raising events, foundations, and a little bit from government. Wealth isn't the great enabler; obedience is. Everyone can do something to make a difference, regardless of how little money he or she has.

"God allowed my childhood to sensitize me and make me available for what I'm doing now. I'm the kind of person who always looks forward, but I try to learn from the past. If I had it to do over again, I would have done Friends a lot earlier. I would have followed my heart sooner. My difficult childhood taught me to be independent, self-reliant, and resourceful. Those are attributes of a successful entrepreneur, so in one sense I know my childhood had a reason. Still, I would not and do not want any child to go through what I did. Friends of the Children is my attempt to keep that from happening."

Wealth isn't the great enabler; obedience is. Everyone can do something to make a difference, regardless of how little money he or she has.

Givers and Receivers
Heather and Keana

KEANA WALKED ACROSS THE STAGE of her elementary school, hugged her principal, and accepted her sixth-grade diploma. Then she turned and ran through a crowded gymnasium straight to Heather, who has been her "Friend" over the past five years.

"You did it, baby!" Heather cried. "You're so beautiful!"

When Heather first met Keana, the troubled child was entering the second grade. Keana had been abandoned by her mother at a neighbor's house in another state, where the four year old stayed for two months. The neighbor eventually contacted Keana's aunt in Portland and sent the child to live with her.

"When I first met Keana, she was very clingy," Heather

remembers. "She was looking for someone to hold onto. I kept telling her I'd be there. I gave her my pager number. I wondered how I could make her understand that I was not going anywhere."

Keana had problems concentrating in school and developing friendships with her peers. She spent long hours in the principal's office and in treatment. She just couldn't seem to hold it together. She would get upset because someone didn't want to stand in line with her, share something with her, or sit with her. She would scream out and hide under her desk. Her teacher warned Heather, "She'll need you a lot."

As Heather spent time each week with Keana, the girl began to show signs of improvement. Heather rewarded accomplishments by taking her out for ice cream, checking out books at the library, or braiding her hair. Sometimes they attended a play or traveled to the Oregon coast. Other times were more informal as Heather showed Keana how to set a table or open a savings account or handle personal hygiene.

"Gradually, things improved," Heather says. "Keana didn't run to the classroom door whenever I showed up. My pager was not going off as often. During her fourth-grade year, I called most mornings to make sure she had done her homework and was heading to school."

The child, once angry and frightened, was handling conflict issues well by the time she reached the fifth grade. She could participate in a group. She had become a team player. "Keana's doing great!" Heather now says proudly. "She's a natural in athletics and ice skating. She's tall, wiry, and has a heart of gold."

In the fall of 1998, Heather asked Keana what she wanted to do after high school.

"I want to play basketball and be a veterinarian," she responded. "And when I'm on the road with the team I'll get someone to watch the animals."

Keana is dreaming big, and Heather is not about to discourage her.

FOR MORE INFORMATION, CONTACT
Friends of the Children
44 N.E. Morris
Portland, OR 97212
503-281-6633
www.friendsofthechildren.com

BOOKS THAT HAVE INFLUENCED DUNCAN CAMPBELL

Joshua and the Children, Joseph Girzone, New York: Simon & Schuster, 1991.

Joshua and the City, Joseph Girzone, New York: Doubleday, 1996.

Golf in the Kingdom, Michael Murphy, New York: Penguin, 1997.

The Sacred Romance: Drawing Closer to the Heart of God, Brent Curtis and John Eldredge, Nashville: Thomas Nelson, 1997.

Sean Lambert became a Christian at the age of sixteen. By the time he was nineteen, Sean felt called into full-time missions. After spending a year at St. John's University in central Minnesota, he joined Youth With A Mission (YWAM), an interdenominational mission agency with more than 15,000 full-time workers at over 650 locations in 135 nations.

For the past quarter century, Sean has touched thousands of lives through various YWAM programs, but none is closer to his heart than Homes of Hope, which builds and gives away houses to the poorest of the poor in Mexico. In 1997 Homes of Hope won the Meritus Civic Award, the highest civic award given by the mayor of Tijuana. Sean and Janet have been married over twenty years. They have three children and live in San Diego, California.

Chapter Eight

Exporting Hope, One House at a Time

Sean Lambert and Homes of Hope

"Give help rather than advice."

Luc de Vauvenargues[1]

Thousands of families in Mexico have little or no housing. The Ramirez family lived underneath a tarp. Pablo is a construction worker and makes thirty-five dollars per week, when he has work. He and his wife, Maria, had eight children until their youngest child died of exposure. One day the government gave them land so they would not be flooded out when the rains came. Through a program called Homes of Hope, a team of Americans and Canadians came to Tijuana and built a home for the Ramirez family. The Americans paid their own expenses, provided the materials, and put up the simple house in a single weekend. They gave it to Pablo and his family as a gift, a testament of God's generous love.

BORDER CROSSING

This heartwarming story has been repeated more than a thousand times in the last dozen years, thanks to the passionate, practical concern of Sean Lambert and his teammates at Youth With A Mission. YWAM, as the group is known, began in 1960 with the vision of Loren Cuningham. Since then, thousands of YWAMers have been involved globally in sharing the love of Christ in word and deed. Sean and Janet Lambert are among that growing number.

"As a teenager, I heard a speaker present the challenge of the unfinished task of world missions," Sean says. "That was just what I wanted to do. I quit college, sold all my stuff, and moved west to join YWAM. My parents thought I was crazy. Now they think it's great."

Along the way, Sean met and married another YWAMer named Janet Izzett in 1981. Together they wound up in Los Angeles, where they spent the next twelve years working with the YWAM training program based there. Sean's duties included helping develop an outreach ministry in Tijuana, Mexico. "Initially, I just wanted a place to take a youth group. I didn't want to go to Tijuana. I thought it wasn't really Mexico, being a border town. But all that changed after I took my first team there in 1990."

Sean remembers that first trip as though it happened yesterday. "The needs absolutely overwhelmed me. Over five thousand people a month move into Tijuana. Many of them end up living under paper lean-tos or in cardboard boxes. Seeing human beings reduced to that just broke my heart."

The seed money that would transform Sean's concern into something concrete came through an unusual set of circumstances, as Sean relates. "When I was in L.A., our director, Dave Gustaveson, wanted to take an offering among the staff. When I asked him what it was for, he said, 'We won't know until after we've taken it. Then we'll pray about what the Lord wants to do with it.' From a staff of forty people we raised 1,500 dollars, but nobody knew what to do with it. I was commuting from L.A. to Tijuana at that time and I met a guy named Sergio Gomez who built houses for the poor. I asked Sergio if we could build a house. He said, 'Sure.' So I went back to L.A. with the idea and everyone thought it was perfect."

Lambert says building that first home was the most fun he's ever had. "Ten of us went to Tijuana, including my two-and-a-half-year-old daughter. We had an absolute blast! As we worked on the house, we noticed a family living in an abandoned bus that had crashed into the nearby hillside. My daughter Andrea kept asking me, 'Daddy, are you going to build a house for that family, too?' That really got to me. So I talked to another youth group when I got back to L.A. about building another house. They jumped all over it. We went down a few months later and constructed a home for the bus family, and Homes of Hope was born. Since then we've just kept going. In April 2002, we finished our one-thousandth home."

Shortly after building its first houses, YWAM rented a permanent facility in the Playas section of Tijuana to house the visiting teams. Then in August of 1991, the Lamberts got permission to start a permanent work in the San Diego/Tijuana area. Along with their three children, they moved south that October. For the next year, they lived with businessman Chris Crane while they got the office and ministry established.

BASIC SHELTER

Sean explains, "There are two theories about community development—crisis intervention and long-term solutions. What Homes of Hope does is primarily crisis intervention. We're dealing with people who are literally sleeping on the ground, getting wet and cold at night. The wonderful thing is that these houses will last fifteen to twenty years if they're taken care of."

Here's how the program works. Homes of Hope selects recipient families who meet three basic criteria: they must have the rights to the land on which the home will be built, they must have at least three children, and their family income must be less than seventy-five dollars per week. Though exceptions exist, the average person who receives a home makes only fifty dollars a month. "There are no home loans in Mexico," says Sean, "unless you are very wealthy. So the only way you can build a house is to pay for it at the time of construction. When we build a house, we give it away. We don't charge the family anything. The people have already bought—or are paying for—the land. That is their commitment, and it's about all they can do.

"About half the homes built go to Christians. The faith of the recipient is not a determining factor. When we build for Christians, we demonstrate the love of God for His children. When we build for nonChristians, we demonstrate His love and mercy for the world. As for the teams that build the houses, we've had atheists, Jewish people, church groups, and business organizations of all kinds. We don't make a big deal of their religious beliefs, but they certainly know what we stand for and what our motivation is."

Groups of ten or more sign up to build a home and pay 3,500 dollars to cover the cost of materials. They spend two or three days on the project. All sorts of teams have come, from youth leaders with their church groups to company presidents with their leadership teams or employees. Many groups have returned to build several homes. "The Disney Corporation has come twice and built ten houses with us," Sean reports. "Mark Zoradi, who is the president of Buena Vista Films Inter-national, told me it was one of the best teambuilding events he's ever experienced. So far we've had over 290 company presidents build homes. Many have come in association with a YPO (Young Presidents' Organization) event. One of the YPO guys asked a Mexican woman what she liked best about her new house. She rolled her eyes and thought. 'Well, now when it rains, it's only wet on the outside.' I started crying when she said that. It's so simple."

We may think we know the best way to do things, but we should have enough humility to learn from those we serve.

Groups are encouraged to bring at least one experienced builder with them, but this isn't required, as Homes of Hope pro-vides a senior builder and on-site coordination. The builder's job is to gauge the group's ability and help them get the job done. Youth groups are given three days per house and adult teams two days. Homes of Hope provides all the plans, tools, and materials to construct a sixteen-foot by twenty-foot house. The homes include a concrete slab, electrical wiring, interior Sheetrock, three windows, and a door. If you ask about a bathroom, Lambert just laughs. "Being Americans we thought, 'Hey, you need a bathroom,' and we included one in our early houses. But the people didn't want it since they had no running water or sewer lines. An outhouse made more sense to them. Now we don't include bath-rooms. We may think we know the best way to do things, but we should have enough humility to learn from those we serve.

"We really have two customers at Homes of Hope," he goes on to say, "one internal and the other external. Our internal cus-tomers are the Mexican families who receive houses. Our exter-nal customers are the Americans and Canadians who come to build them. The beauty of what we're doing is that it's a complete turnkey operation. We make it easy for people to get involved. We pick up the teams at the airport. We feed and house them. We give them all the tools and materials. We pour the slab before they arrive. They just show up and build the house."

Some have compared Homes of Hope to Habitat for Human-ity, a much larger and more well-known program based in Atlanta. Sean has great respect for Habitat. "They're doing a wonderful job. I think Habitat is awesome. But they're building much more com-plicated houses for people who can afford a monthly payment. Their homes in Mexico have 150- to 200-dollar monthly payments, which is a month's wages for an average Mexican worker. We are building houses for the poorest of the poor, folks who could never afford that kind of payment."

BOOMING PROGRAM

Sean Lambert describes himself as an entrepreneur. "I like the chal-lenge of growing something. Early on I wanted to see fifty houses built a year. In 2001 we put up 208. The year before that we did 162. We are doubling in size every couple of years. To date we've built more than a thousand homes in Tijuana, Ensenada, Guadala-jara, Culiacán, Juarez, and Cancun, one of the fastest growing cities in Mexico.

"At first I tried to do everything myself. Our first year we did a handful of houses and I helped on most of them. But now that we're doing so many homes, I'm only able to be hands-on with six or eight annually. I've had to change my leadership style. I now focus on creating opportunities to involve others."

As with most businesses or ministries, "our early years were difficult," Lambert remembers. "We had a lot of challenges to overcome, but through it all God proved faithful. Today we have a 4,000-square-foot office and warehouse in San Diego that serves as our administrative center. We also have two outreach centers in Northern Baja, Mexico. In 2001 we hosted 6,000 participants from 300 different groups."

Many ministries start out with passion, but then devolve into bureaucracies in which the program runs the people. Not so with Homes of Hope. It remains a labor of love performed by volunteers who not only do the work but also pay for the privilege, as Sean explains. "We only build houses when groups show up and say, 'Here's our 3,500 dollars for materials and team costs. When do we start?' The groups not only pay for everything, they're the ones who come and do the work. It's a cool deal. The cost hasn't slowed down the pace. If anything, our model is too successful. We have to turn down hundreds of people a year who want to build houses because we don't have the staff or infrastructure to handle them."

When you give a check, something is drawn from your account; but when you give of yourself, something is deposited in you.

Those who do come to build a home are changed by the experience, as Sean has witnessed time and again. "Often when people see poverty up close, it overwhelms them. They don't know what to do about it. What we provide is a simple, hands-on way to do something tangible, something that causes the 'giver' to come away more blessed than the 'receiver.' My theory is that because we are created in the image of God, and He is a giver, we are wired to be givers. When we help others, we're happy and fulfilled because that's how we're designed. Our program provides an opportunity for people to give of themselves, to go beyond writing a check and actually do something with their own hands."

Tim Talbott, now a Homes of Hope board member, put it this way: "When you give a check, something is drawn from your account; but when you give of yourself, something is deposited in you." "Here's this executive who perhaps has never used a hammer in his life," Sean elaborates. "He brings his wife and kids and they hammer and paint together for a few days and when they're finished, they've built a house. They get dirty and tired by the time they go home, but it's been worth it to make a difference for one family."

"Homes of Hope was an answer to my prayer for a family mission trip," says Kevin Jenkins, former president and CEO of Canadian Airlines.

> I was looking for more than just a tour of an underdeveloped country. I wanted something that permitted all the members of my family to put their faith into action by serving others in great need. We loved the experience! Our kids loved it so much that they have initiated a number of return visits. After building our first house our oldest son said, "I've never built anything that someone else could use before!"[2]

Sean is a realist about human nature. "When it comes to the daunting task of helping the poor, start small. Those who do too much too soon often get discouraged and quit. You can increase your involvement down the road. And once you decide what you want to do—build houses, for instance—it's just as important to know what you are not supposed to do. There are perimeters that come with a clear focus."

When it comes to the daunting task of helping the poor, start small. Those who do too much too soon often get discouraged and quit.

After so many years in ministry, Sean's heart is still tender and easily broken. "I weep for the people in Tijuana and other Mexican cities," he says, "yet what we're doing there through Homes of Hope isn't a burden. When the love of God overwhelms you, the response is joy, not work. It's a pleasure, not a sacrifice. For me it's a lot of fun. You couldn't pay me to do anything else."

However, God does promise to reward those who care for the poor in practical ways:

> Is not this the kind of fasting I have chosen: . . .Is it not to share your food with the hungry and to provide the poor wanderer with shelter—when you see the naked, to clothe him, and not to turn away from your own flesh and blood? Then your light will break forth like the dawn, and your healing will quickly appear; then your righteousness will go before you, and the glory of the Lord will be your rear guard (Isaiah 58:6-8).

No wonder Sean is so thrilled about what he's doing.

Givers and Receivers
Mike Kemper

IT ALL STARTED FOR US in December 1998—our first trip to build homes for the poor. The YPO Fellowship Focus Forum invited us. We went to give some of our time instead of just some of our money. We went because we knew God had blessed us abundantly and we wanted to help others. Little did we know what blessings we'd be receiving.

Friday night we met the people from YWAM. We experienced Sean and his staff as they smoothly and lovingly navigated us through a weekend that literally changed lives, and not just the lives of the family that got a new home. We expected them to be ecstatic about their new house, but we didn't expect their tears and prayers of joy as we presented them with the keys to their new Home of Hope. We expected the neighbors to be jealous, not for them to graciously help build the house.

We hoped our kids would become more grateful for what they have, but never expected them to realize how their financial blessings carry a burden of responsibility to work hard and not miss opportunities to help others. We hoped they would play with the local kids, but were thrilled when they saw that these kids' happiness was not a function of the amount of money they had. We prayed we would all learn to value those in poverty by seeing them as human beings made in God's image. Our prayers were answered by seeing that their poverty frees them up to be less materialistic and self-conscious and more genuine and unselfish.

We wanted our family to draw closer together because we worked together, never expecting to become closer because the God who loves and cares for us, even in dire circumstances, drew us closer to Him. Our kids left wanting to start a club at school in order to bring other kids back for the experience. We have since gone back five times and have brought friends and relatives.

FOR MORE INFORMATION, CONTACT
Homes of Hope
100 West 35th Street, Suite C
National City, CA 91950
619-420-1900
www.ywamsandiegobaja.org

BOOKS THAT HAVE INFLUENCED SEAN LAMBERT
Developing the Leader Within You, John C. Maxwell, Nashville: Thomas Nelson, 2001.

Spiritual Leadership, J. Oswald Chambers, Chicago: Moody Press, 1974.

The E-Myth Revisited: Why Most Small Businesses Don't Work and What to Do About It, Michael E. Gerber, New York: HarperBusiness, 1995.

Selling the Invisible: A Field Guide to Modern Marketing, Harry Beckwell, New York: Warner Books, 1997.

The 21 Irrefutable Laws of Leadership: Becoming the Person Others Will Want to Follow, John C. Maxwell, Nashville: Thomas Nelson, 1999.

Kit Danley has almost seven hundred children, two by natural birth and the rest adopted. Through Neighborhood Ministries, which she helped found in 1982, she brings the love of Christ to inner city kids and their families. She is a past recipient of The 100 Phoenix Best—Volunteer Award. Her work has received national attention and has been featured in various articles, including "The 100 Best Things the Church is Doing" in *Christianity Today*.

Kit is a speaker for Perspectives International, the Richard Devos Urban Leadership Initiative, and the Hispanic Ministry Center. She has served as a board member of The Fuller Seminary Extension Board and on the executive committee for the Luis Palau Crusade. She and her husband, Wayne, have lived, ministered, and raised their two children in the inner city of Phoenix for twenty-five years.

Chapter Nine

THE POWER OF A MOTHER'S LOVE

Kit Danley and Neighborhood Ministries

"It is easy to love people who are far away but it is not always so easy to love those who live with us or right next to us. I do not agree with the big way of doing things— love needs to start with an individual."

Mother Teresa[1]

Arizona has more than its share of the rich and famous. But where there's sun, there are also shadows. According to the *2001 Kids Count Data Book*, Arizona ranks forty-fifth in the nation for the welfare of its children and thirty-seventh for the percentage of kids living in poverty. The median income of its families is 18 percent below the national average. It ranks forty-eighth in the number of babies born to teenagers. In addition to high teen suicide and homicide rates, Arizona also has the highest percentage of high school dropouts and one of the highest percentages of teens not in school and not working.[2]

Since 1982, Neighborhood Ministries has been working in the dark places in the Valley of the Sun. Kit Danley, Neighborhood's founder, says, "Living in the community we serve, we long to be the shining presence of Christ. We are the arms of Jesus embracing children and families who are looking for hope, healing, and love."

OFF THE LAKE

Kit grew up in Milwaukee, the oldest of three children. "Both sides of my family come from off the lake," she says, "meaning they were wealthy. My parents traveled in affluent, high-society circles, but both struggled with personal issues, and when I was seven, my father killed himself. Our home was nominally Episcopalian. The priest at our church was 'born-again' and often led parishioners to Christ. Church life became painful for him because of political pressure and he eventually left. Before he did, his wife shared the good news with her Sunday school class, and it was there that I believed the gospel.

"However," Kit continues, "I lived in a pagan environment and, as a preteen, I started carousing and running the streets. In high school I attended Young Life, yet I had trust issues with God. I'd received him as Savior, but I didn't want Him messing with my life or telling me what to do. After graduation I went to Colorado College, my dad's alma mater and a school my grandfather had given a lot of money to. While there, I began to realize that a Christian is someone who lives for Christ. But by now I had a new stumbling block to keep me from following Him—human suffering. If God is so loving, why is there so much suffering?

> *"The way I care for the poor," Jesus said, "is by working through people who hear My heart and take My love into difficult places."*

"This seems an odd concern for a child from an affluent background," Danley admits, "but I was horrifically aware this planet was dying in pain. Perhaps this was such an issue for me because I was dying of pain. I had a lot of heartaches. My family was as dysfunctional as any inner-city family. Having been raised in what I call the underside of affluence, I knew firsthand the incredible poverty and pain there can be in materialism.

In the midst of her turmoil, the Lord spoke into Kit's life through a brother in Christ. "He shared Luke 12:48 with me, 'To those who are given much, much is required.' This truth hit me like a powerful spiritual wind. I surrendered my life completely to Christ and heard Him say, 'Kit, there is no question too big for me. You care about the suffering of the planet and so do I. 'The way I care for the poor,' Jesus said, 'is by working through people who hear My heart and take My love into difficult places.' This calling was so huge I couldn't avoid it. It was a very specific call to reach out to my community.

"Like a lot of kids in the early '70s, I wanted to find meaning in life. Now I had a sense of purpose and significance, a reason for being. I started Bible studies and began sharing my faith. I got involved with a group called Campus Ambassadors. We were discipled by incredible people like Vernon Grounds, Rufus Jones, and Don Davis. I learned about God's heart for the poor, which became evident as I discovered there are over four hundred passages and more than a thousand verses dealing with the poor in Scripture."

Danley didn't drop out of school and hit the streets. Instead, she completed her sociology degree at Northern Arizona University in Flagstaff. "I had planned to return to Denver, where I had done an internship in inner-city ministry, but God had other plans. I fell in love with a man who had been a friend for years. Wayne and I got married in 1978 and I eventually went to work with him and another friend, Bill Thrall, in a ministry called Hand and Hand. It was part of Open Door Fellowship in Phoenix."

The rest is history. Open Door bought a building in a low-income, multi-ethnic, Phoenix neighborhood in 1981. Within a year, Wayne and Kit moved their young family into that neighborhood—their kids were four and one at the time—and they've lived there ever since.

INTO THE CITY

"The call to live in the inner city is something you have to be convinced of as husband and wife," Kit stresses. "It can be dangerous. Our kids went to inner-city schools as part of a 2-percent white minority. When we moved in, our house had no outside doors that locked and twenty-six broken windows. We were stepping out in faith, believing in the vision of a local church showing their community what Jesus looked like with skin on."

"Certainly, love is expressed first in being *with* before doing *to* someone," writes Mother Teresa in *A Simple Path*.

If our actions do not first come from the desire to be with a person, then it really becomes just social work. When you are willing to be with a poor person you can recognize his need and if your love is genuine you naturally want to do what you can as an expression of your love. Service, in a way, is simply a means of expressing your being for that person—and often with the poorest people you cannot completely alleviate their problem. But by being with them, by being for them, whatever you can do for them makes a difference.[3]

The Danleys not only moved into the inner city, but the inner city moved in with them. "Over the years," writes David Holmstrom in *The Christian Science Monitor*, "Danley and her family have taken in dozens of young people and even families." Holmstrom sites several examples, such as,

Victor Lopez, a fifteen year old on probation, [who] was recently released to Danley's custody. Danley has known Victor and his family since he was a small boy. Mr. Lopez has been in and out of juvenile detention as a gang member. His brother was killed in a gang incident. His father died of alcoholism at a young age, and his mother and sisters are living on an Indian reservation. Victor is also the father of a baby.[4]

This story illustrates Kit's long-term commitment to the community she loves. "People wanting to be true change-agents in distressed communities should plan on moving in and staying awhile," she says. "We came to stay, but we weren't on our own. We were part of a caring group of believers. The elders at Open Door Fellowship realized the needs of our neighbors would press in on our church. Somebody would have to address them. That's why they asked me to design a neighborhood ministry. For the first seven or eight years we functioned as part of Open Door. We called ourselves the Food and Clothing Bank Ministry, then the Urban Ministry, and finally Neighborhood Ministries. We became a separate nonprofit ministry in 1992. This allowed us to partner with other churches wanting to work in the city."

The Food and Clothing Bank was one of the first church-based food banks in Phoenix. But Kit and her coworkers didn't stop there. "Soon our teams began visiting food bank recipients and helping them in various ways. As more Spanish-speaking women frequented the food bank, we began Spanish Bible studies, which grew into a Spanish-speaking church—*Iglesia Nueva Esperanza.* One of their first converts now pastors this growing church. We also began an outreach to Hispanic children called Neighborhood Kids Club. We've added a school-year outreach called Kids Life and a similar program for teens. To increase the academic chances of the most at-risk children, we began a tutoring ministry called Partners in Learning. We've also created summer camping and winter retreats for the city kids."

People wanting to be true change-agents in distressed communities should plan on moving in and staying awhile.

Neighborhood Ministries' programs are diverse and dynamic, yet they are all based on a clear sense of what the ministry is about. "We invest in long-term relationships," Danley declares. "We stay involved in people's lives for as long as they allow us to. We track transient families, encouraging them to stay involved in our programs."

"Danley starts early with the children," Amy Sherman reports in *Christianity Today,* "tenaciously tracking them as they move from one dilapidated apartment to another—sometimes ten to twelve moves in a year (three to five times, Kit now says). . . .'We don't want to just snatch a kid out of a gang. We want to start early enough in the child's life that he makes a decision not to join gangs at all.'"[5]

The ministry doesn't give up on throwaway kids, the ones that most people have decided aren't worth the effort. They aggressively intervene when kids are trapped in self-destructive behaviors. "Our programs become refuges for children and teens from the horrors of drive-by shootings, drugs, street life, and the instability that's so common in their lives," Kit says. "Our tutoring, mentoring, jail visitation, and biblical counseling programs give them the help they need to survive and succeed."

Danley likes to emphasize that a big part of the calling of Neighborhood Ministries is to mentor indigenous leaders. "Through faithful friendships over the long haul we help people discover and develop their God-given gifts and abilities. We emphasize character development and servant leadership. One thing we won't do is patronize. We don't want to be a disempowering organization, one that creates more dependency among the poor."

Estean Lenyoun, cofounder of Impact Urban America in San Diego, agrees with this approach. "Our programs are geared to empower people, not to foster dependency on others, especially the government." Lenyoun decries what he calls neo-plantationalism—"government programs and welfare handouts that keep people at a certain level of dependency. What the people are really looking for is tough love and accountability. They want hope and dignity, which must be earned; it can't just be given."[6]

FROM ORGANISM TO ORGANIZATION

When the Lord prospers a vision, the subsequent growth leads to transition. There are costs and adjustments to make in evolving from an organism into an organization. "If your ministry gets large, as ours has," Kit explains, "you can't live in la-la land. You need infrastructure in order to be healthy. My natural inclination is to be cautious of structure. I don't want it to overshadow the vision and eventually create an organizational shell to be kept in place. However, as an old sociology major, I know the importance of structure."

Starbuck's CEO, Howard Schultz, speaks of this tension in his book *Pour Your Heart Into It*:

> If you're a creative person, an entrepreneur at heart, introducing systems and bureaucracies can be painful, for they seem like the antithesis of what attracted you to business

[or ministry] in the first place. But if you don't institute the right processes, if you don't coordinate and plan, if you don't hire people with MBA skills, the whole edifice could crumble.[7]

"The Lord has led us every step of the way," says Kit, "still, I constantly pray, 'God, help us to be faithful in building an infrastructure that allows our passion and vision to move forward.' We started as an outreach of a local church, but now we own eight acres and have buildings to build and money to raise. I don't know what we would have done without the skilled people the Lord has brought along to help us, especially on the board level. Our board has had to become a working board versus an advisory board. We have a member who does all the infrastructure development work for one of the largest medical insurance companies in Arizona. We also have a city planner, as well as a property developer and a civil engineer. I'm availing myself of their expertise rather than trying to learn everything myself."

Business-minded people have to submit to their ministry partners before they will be trusted and allowed to bring their skills to the table.

But skills are only part of the equation. Kit believes the Neighborhood board works so well because its members are submissive to the cultural context of the ministry. "These businesspeople love this work," she stresses. "They've never judged it for being messy, for being too relational, for not watching the bottom line closely enough. This doesn't mean they don't ask the hard questions when appropriate, though, or hesitate to apply their business acumen where needed."

How they assert those skills is critical, Danley maintains. "Business-minded people have to submit to their ministry partners before they will be trusted and allowed to bring their skills to the table. As outsiders, they aren't going to initially understand the culture inside a ministry. It's going to feel far too relational, far too messy.

They have to become teachable in order to become effective.

While she lives and works in the bustling inner city, Kit confesses to being a bit of a Christian mystic with a strong attraction to the contemplative life. "I enjoy getting alone with the Lord and I do a lot of hiking for prayer. It puts me in mind of what Douglas Steere refers to as, 'The realization that one is personally expendable for the work of the kingdom. . .the knowledge that life is lent to be spent.'"

Kit is choosing to spend her life a day at a time serving the One who said, "I tell you the truth, whatever you did for one of the least of these brothers of mine, you did for me" (Matthew 25:40).

Givers and Receivers
Luis Osoy

LUIS OSOY GREW UP in Guatemala City, where as a youngster he sold drugs and earned a reputation as a violent gang leader. In 1989 he moved to Phoenix and continued his criminal activities. But his heart hungered for something more. Through his nephew, Luis met Jeff Kanner, a man who had what Luis wanted—love. Jeff lived with the Danleys at the time and attended Open Door Fellowship.

"One day I rode my bike to Kit Danley's house," Luis remembers. "I didn't go in. I just tried to see Jeff through the window. I kept thinking, 'Why is that guy like that? What is different about these people?' And I began to cry."

Even if he wanted to change, Luis doubted he could break away from the gang lifestyle. "When you're a drug dealer, you can't just quit. If you do, something terrible will happen to you. You'll wind up dead." But when all the members of his gang were arrested, Luis felt free to spend more time with Jeff and other Christians who offered their friendship.

"They talked a lot about God's love," Osoy recalls, "but to a gangster, love is a gross word."

But, gross or not, love prevailed. And in the end, alone in his apartment, Luis surrendered his life to Christ. Today he works as a volunteer with Neighborhood Ministries in their Kids Life program. "I like to hang out with gangsters," he says. "Every gang member has the same spiritual needs as I did. I made the mistake of trying to fill those needs through a gang. It took me years to realize I was wrong. I learned my lesson the hard way, but I'm living proof to others that there is a way out of gang life.

"Neighborhood Ministries is providing so many good choices for all those who come here," Luis continues. "A good example is the variety of activities we have on Monday night. The kids learn about God, learn to dream—to think about what they want to be when they grow up—to believe that there will be a tomorrow. They learn that there is hope for them.

"I love working with these kids," Luis says with a smile. "When I see a needy kid, I see myself as a child always looking for acceptance, love, and hope. After I became a Christian, I decided to share Christ's love with the ones who don't know Him. This isn't easy because most of them don't know what love really means. But I know God can change all that. I know it's possible to have a new life because it's happened to me!"

FOR MORE INFORMATION, CONTACT
Neighborhood Ministries
1918 W. Van Buren Street
Phoenix, AZ 85009
602-252-5225
www.neighborhoodministries.org

BOOKS THAT HAVE INFLUENCED KIT DANLEY
Companion to the Poor, Viv Grigg, Sydney, Australia: Albatross Books, 1984.
Restorers of Hope, Amy Sherman, Wheaton, Ill.: Crossway Books, 1997.
Focused Lives, Dr. J. Robert Clinton, Altadena, Calif.: Barnabas Publishers, 1995.
Good News to the Poor, Walter E. Pilgrim, Minneapolis: Augsburg Publishing House, 1981.
Disciplines for the Inner Life, Bob Benson, Sr. and Michael W. Benson, Nashville: Thomas Nelson, 1989.
With Justice for All, John Perkins, Ventura, Calif.: Regal Books, 1982.

Larry Donnithorne has served for more than thirty years in leadership positions in educational and engineering settings. He earned an Ed.D. in higher education administration from Harvard, an M.S. in civil engineering and an M.A. in economics from Stanford, and a B.S. in general engineering from the U.S. Military Academy at West Point. For thirteen years he was a teacher and administrator at the Point and served as the Academy's senior strategic planner.

In 1993, Colonel Donnithorne retired from the military and became president of the College of the Albemarle in North Carolina. Then in 1998 he accepted the presidency of Colorado Christian University near Denver. He is the author of *The West Point Way of Leadership*. Larry and Fran Donnithorne have been married more than thirty years and have four grown children.

Chapter Ten

HOW "HIGH" SHOULD HIGHER LEARNING GO?

Larry Donnithorne and Colorado Christian University

"Religion is a social concern, for it operates powerfully on society, contributing, in various ways, to its stability and prosperity. Religion is not merely a private affair; the community is deeply interested in its diffusion; for it is the best support of the virtues and principles on which the social order rests."

William Holmes McGuffey[1]

An entrepreneur is someone who gets something new done, says Peter Drucker, but this doesn't necessarily mean starting something new. Larry Donnithorne is an example of the growing number of social entrepreneurs who choose to make their marks through well-established institutions instead of starting something original. And few segments of American society are more institutionalized than higher education. Fewer still have a more strategic impact on the future, and Donnithorne is nothing if not a strategic thinker. He's a former senior strategic planner for the U.S. Military Academy at West Point.

> *An entrepreneur is someone who gets something new done, but this doesn't necessarily mean starting something new.*

When Colonel Donnithorne retired from a distinguished military career, he had many choices within academia. His curriculum vitae included degrees from Harvard, Stanford, and West Point. In 1998, he chose the presidency of one of the smallest NCAA

Division II schools in the country. Colorado Christian University is an evangelical liberal arts school nestled in the foothills of the Rocky Mountains near Denver. The only member of the Council of Christian Colleges and Universities in an eight-state region, CCU has more than a thousand resident undergraduate students and about two thousand students in other programs.

So, what is Donnithorne doing at a small Christian college in Colorado? Learning to snowboard for one thing, but primarily helping young people learn how biblical faith makes sense in the modern world.

JOURNEY OF FAITH

Larry's commitment to education grows out of his commitment to Christ. "My Christian faith is the context for my life," he says. "I was raised in a Christian home and confirmed in the First Methodist Church of Lubbock, Texas. But during my college years I came under the influence of secular philosophy. I rejected my faith for a time due to intellectual pride. I continued to ignore my faith for years—until the night I witnessed the birth of my first child.

"In the months afterward, I admitted to myself that my worldview didn't satisfy. I began a serious inquiry into the world's major faiths. About this time a friend invited me to a Bible study. There I heard again, as if for the first time, the claim that in the Scripture, God had given a trustworthy self-revelation. I studied that proposition for months and found grounds for an intellectual belief in God."

Soon, however, Larry learned that God wanted more than his mind. "Revelation imposes a responsibility to respond with one's whole life," he notes. "For a time I felt a strong urge to attend seminary and train for the ministry. Eventually I decided my calling was to live out my faith as a layman." Much of his journey of faith took place against a background of drab green. After high school graduation, he got an appointment to West Point. He graduated in 1966 as a second lieutenant and went through Airborne Training and Ranger School before Uncle Sam sent him to Vietnam in 1968.

Upon returning to the States, Donnithorne picked up two

degrees from Stanford and worked as a civil engineer. He remembers himself as "an aggressive, ambitious army officer in the Corps of Engineers with designs on making the rank of General and Chief of Engineers. I was committed to the engineering world, to building roads, bridges, buildings, and airfields. But as I came to appreciate the value of people, I became more interested in the social sciences and the humanities. I went back to West Point to teach in 1976. I discovered I really liked building people more than buildings. I was selected for the tenured faculty at West Point, which first took me to Harvard to finish my doctorate. I also served a two-year tour of duty in Korea from 1979 to 1981."

Donnithorne spent thirteen years at West Point. After retiring, he decided to throw his hat in the ring for a couple of small college presidencies and wound up at the College of the Albemarle in North Carolina. "In my sixth year at the College of the Albemarle," Donnithorne recalls, "I felt the urge to move on. I wanted someplace where I would be freer to implement my vision of educating the whole person. At West Point, I was able to work on character development and leadership development in addition to cognitive development. At the community college, I had to be much more sensitive to the separation of church and state."

West Point doesn't have the kind of church-state separation found in society. The courts have upheld the value of promoting spiritual life within the armed services. There's a Chaplains' Corp, and public monies are used to build chapels and to foster spiritual life among cadets. Donnithorne says, "It's only logical that our military leaders need to be men and women with deep moral foundations. But at the community college, I felt that we were educating with one hand tied behind our backs. We could address only the mind and hands—knowledge and skills, but not the heart.

"About this time, Bob Andringa, president for the Council of Christian Colleges and Universities, nominated me for the presidency of CCU. This happened just after a visit to Colorado with my wife, which led us to think such a move might be from God. I accepted the position in the summer of 1998."

PHILOSOPHY OF EDUCATION

According to Scott Adams, the acclaimed creator of the Dilbert comic,

> There are only two types of educations, useful and useless. If you're foolish enough to get one of those useful educations, such as an engineering degree, everything you learn will be obsolete in five years. The rest of what you learn for the remainder of your life will come from reading brochures from vendors. That's why I majored in economics. With economics, you never have to worry that your degree will become less relevant over time. I mean, how…could it?[2]

Donnithorne's perspective on education is a bit different. "Education is a profound opportunity to make a difference in people's lives. What the human race becomes is, in large measure, a product of how we educate our young. God should be involved in this process. He doesn't force Himself on us, however, but gives us freedom to form ourselves by our choices and our children by education.

"My philosophy of education is built on a high regard for truth," Larry continues, "and the pursuit of sound reasons for all beliefs. This is coupled with a humility that acknowledges our limitations to comprehend truth apart from divine inspiration. Because all truth is God's truth, we can be encouraged to search for, and consider, truth-claims wherever they may be found. The ultimate test is consistency within the overarching framework of Christian beliefs."

Education is a profound opportunity to make a difference in people's lives. . . .God should be involved in this process.

Donnithorne is convinced that "the orthodox biblical faith is true. It will withstand any fair-minded intellectual scrutiny. I believe God honors the sincere inquirer's need for intellectual ground from which to take a step of personal faith. Even atheists and agnostic scientists must rely *in faith* on the plausibility of their theories—and they often do so with less evidence for their beliefs than Christians have.

"The ultimate goal of education is transformation," says Donnithorne. "The educational continuum moves from indoctrination to education to transformation. Some colleges only *indoctrinate*. They believe they have a lock on the truth and they simply teach young people to parrot it. *Education* rejects that approach, insisting the fundamental questions in life just can't be conclusively answered. Still, one can build a strong inductive case for those important things, even though people may build their cases differently. An educational institution should represent a variety of viewpoints that force students to decide for themselves what is true and what they will live by. Finally, there should be an experience of *transformation* that takes people from living for themselves to living for God. That's where the ultimate satisfaction is found. If students leave college prepared to spend their lives serving God, they've experienced a transformation."

The president of CCU says his school "is not a place where all ideas are equal, as in secular institutions. But, at the other end of the spectrum, we're not an institution where only one set of ideas is accepted. Rather, within the bounds of the historic, orthodox, evangelical faith, we insist upon genuine scholarship and debate. We believe in the freedom to continue to disagree and to seek greater light and understanding through interaction as scholars.

"I believe the Christian framework is the only one that makes complete sense of the world," says Larry. "Within this framework we have to be thoughtful Christians, humbly aware of our limitations but still seeking to discern what is true. We also have to learn how to handle the revelation of God—in Christ, in Scripture, and in creation—and use it to help build a society that's honoring to Him. For years, many institutions of higher education have been distancing themselves from their spiritual roots. This is a tragic mistake because it leads to an incomplete education. I want to do just the opposite.

"A Christ-centered education is a complete education,"

Donnithorne insists. "Secular and Christian institutions teach many of the same core subjects—languages, sciences, the humanities. However, in the secular setting, professors oppose discussion of a larger spiritual framework that makes sense of all these topics. Their courses are like the jumbled pieces of a jigsaw puzzle dumped out of the box. But in a Christ-centered education, the pieces fit together, bringing coherence to the educational experience and providing a structure for lifelong learning. A sound and rigorous Christ-centered education (not indoctrination!) should strengthen and deepen personal faith. To that end, students at CCU study secular disciplines with Christian professors who have integrated their biblical faith with those disciplines."

How does Donnithorne answer those who say going to a Christian university is withdrawing from the world into a hothouse environment? "There's a place for both Christian and secular institutions," he maintains. "Some young people whose faith is very well-developed can withstand the challenges that exist in a secular institution. But the primary impact of a secular institution will be to secularize one's outlook. I suspect that most young people who are serious about their Christianity still have a maturing faith that needs strengthening before it can handle the challenges of secular education and life." Having said this, he does not subscribe to a division between the spiritual and the secular. "Everything a Christian does is sacred. If I permit God to work through me, He can accomplish His purposes whether I'm in a secular business setting or leading a Christian ministry. As a school, we are equally committed to preparing students for the pastorate or for teaching in the public schools or for going into business."

Contrary to some perceptions of the concept of fundamentalism, Donnithorne asserts, "We are a liberal arts university. I interpret 'liberal' to imply an education that's liberating. It liberates the learner from a blind reliance on the opinions and dictates of others. The aims of such an education are threefold: first, to provide a broad and integrated understanding of the major areas of inquiry; second, to give one the power to reason logically and communicate effectively; third, to lay a groundwork for developing a personal ethic. The reason for the founding of higher education in America in the first place was to supply a liberal education to Christian ministers. Such an education is still appropriate today. Higher education can be academically sound and demanding and at the same time enthusiastically Christian. These qualities aren't mutually exclusive."

On that point, Donnithorne would agree with Samuel Huntington, a professor at Harvard and director of the John M. Olin Institute for Strategic Studies, who wrote: "Western Christianity, first Catholicism and then Protestantism, is the single most important historical characteristic of Western civilization. Indeed, during most of its first millennium, what is now known as Western civilization was called Western Christendom."[3]

ATTITUDE OF RESPECT

Working in a Christian setting doesn't mean everything is heavenly. "When I made the move to CCU," Larry recalls, "a gentleman who had been at West Point and who then worked at a Christian college gave me some advice. 'Be careful about moving into Christian higher education. Don't expect it to be idyllic.' I now understand what he meant.

"Initially, I failed to recognize how dogmatic and intolerant Christians can be when they disagree on issues they perceive to be major. Christians need a degree of humility regarding our ability to comprehend an infinite God; but, more importantly, we need to unite in our love of God in order to reach a culture in desperate need of what we've found. Yet, we are busy criticizing and fighting with each other. I've been appalled by the lack of charity among Christians. We feel strongly about our convictions and are unwilling to hold them with any degree of humility. This intolerance seems to be fueled primarily by confusion about revelation and whether it enables us to have total comprehension of 'the truth.' We fail to see that while our Bibles are wholly trustworthy, our human interpretations of them may not be. Christians need to hold two concepts in equal tension: that our core beliefs about God are worth dying for, while at the same time we are limited, fallible beings who therefore owe charity toward people who disagree with us. We should be prepared to offer the reasons for our own convictions and, in turn, to grant others the honor of respect for the reasons for their convictions."

Still, Donnithorne emphasizes the upside of a Christian environment. "We have an advantage in that we share a basic spiritual framework. We see each other as members of a body of believers so we can work through our difficulties with a shared understanding."

Being a university president means more than educating. It involves leadership, a subject Donnithorne has written about in his book *The West Point Way of Leadership.* "I spent many years at West Point teaching and thinking about the process of leadership development as well as facilitating the moral development of cadets. What I learned there also applies to a Christian college, which is in the business of spiritual leadership development. My leadership style is grounded in my faith. I have a fundamental respect for people based on their being created in God's image. A leader should enable the members of the organization to succeed in their roles. If people succeed, the organization succeeds."

A leader should enable the members of the organization to succeed in their roles. If people succeed, the organization succeeds.

Because of this high valuation of people, Donnithorne tries to hire talented men and women and then gives them wide latitude in which to work. "I trust them to do their jobs responsibly until they give me cause to doubt them," he says. "While at times we will decide jointly *what* must be done, I trust them to decide *how* to get it done. As General George Patton once said, 'Never tell people how to do things. Tell them what to do and they will surprise you with their ingenuity.'"

In his book, Donnithorne quotes another famous general on the subject of getting the best from people.

The greatest challenge leaders face is to show that they care deeply about both accomplishing the mission and the people who accomplish it. The leader's true effectiveness arises largely from a sincere regard for each member of the team. General Omar Bradley wrote, "A leader should possess human understanding and consideration for others. People are not robots and should not be treated as such. I do not by any means suggest coddling. But people are intelligent, complicated beings who will respond favorably to human understanding and consideration. By these means their leader will get maximum effort from each of them. He will also get loyalty."[4]

Larry Donnithorne is a driven man. And what drives him is the thought of equipping a generation of "world changers," young followers of Jesus who are so centered on God that they will, through Him, change their culture and world. "My ambition is to love God," Larry states emphatically, "and to serve Him by investing my energy in the development of others. He's provided me with the gifts, talents, and experience to pursue this ambition within Christian higher education.

"I see my life as having two continuing purposes," he concludes. "First, to cooperate with God's good purposes for my own growth as His child. And, second, to serve Him as a willing vessel through whom He can work in the lives of others."

Such an attitude gets an "A" in God's book.

Givers and Receivers
David Anderson

I CAME TO COLORADO CHRISTIAN UNIVERSITY from a farm in southwest Minnesota. It was at CCU that God began to grip my life in powerful ways. During my freshman year I remember praying, "God, I love this place, but please don't let me be in leadership. Call me to preach or evangelize, but let someone else lead." But as I got immersed in campus life, it was almost impossible not to get involved. There were opportunities left and right. Ministries, clubs, organizations. Everywhere I turned I saw chances to get connected with people, and God began using these to shape and prepare me for the road ahead.

Soon I found myself nominated and accepted into the school's four-year leadership program. This opened the floodgates of opportunity even farther. One day a faculty member and the VP of Student Life asked me to start a ministry called True North, which I did. Later I was nominated to be student body president. I laughed in recollection of my earlier prayers, but went ahead and ran because I sensed God wanted me to. I won the election and as president I had the privilege of working with forty-five paid staff as well as 170 other faculty and student leaders. The experience was invaluable!

My time at CCU gave me the chance to learn and mature in a community that fostered spiritual growth. I had great mentors who walked alongside me and helped me make decisions about my future. The professors did a very good job of integrating Scripture into various fields of learning. I studied liberal arts with one hand on the Bible and the other on a newspaper or book, and came away with the tools I need to function in a pluralistic world. I've learned how to think for myself in the light of God's Word.

Graduating from CCU has been bittersweet for me as I cut my umbilical cord of CCU life. As I reflect on my years at CCU, it brings me both sorrow and joy. Sorrow in a sense that I had to leave some of my best friends. I had to say good-bye to a unique form of community that can only be compared to the Eternal. And joy in that I know CCU is being carried on by men and women who are serious about their relationship with Jesus Christ and are not about to let the world drag them down. I have been able to watch freshmen, sophomores, and juniors, whom I knew from day one, develop into godly men and women, and I look upward and give thanks to God. Indeed, He has blessed this place.

FOR MORE INFORMATION, CONTACT
Colorado Christian University
180 S. Garrison Street
Lakewood, CO 80226
303-963-3399
www.ccu.edu

BOOKS THAT HAVE INFLUENCED LARRY DONNITHORNE
The Knowledge of the Holy, A. W. Tozer, San Francisco: Harper, 1978.

Knowing God, J. I. Packer, Downers Grove, Ill.: InterVarsity Press, 1973.

The Message of the Sermon on the Mount, John Stott, Downers Grove, Ill.: InterVarsity Press, 1988.

The Spirit of the Disciplines: Understanding How God Changes Lives, Dallas Willard, San Francisco: Harper Collins, 1988.

Mere Christianity, C. S. Lewis, New York: Macmillan, 1952.

God in the Dock, C. S. Lewis, Grand Rapids, Mich.: Eerdmans, 1994.

Fred Peterson is a native of South Dakota and the product of a godly home. He graduated from Northwestern College in Minneapolis in 1964 and took a job as director of an inner-city program in Minneapolis. Later he taught for a year at the Bar None Ranch for Boys before he and his wife, Dorothy, joined the Peace Corps and moved to the West Indies.

After returning to Minnesota, Fred taught for a year in the Robbinsdale school district. He then went to Philadelphia and taught at another residential treatment center for delinquent boys. After earning his master's degree, he returned to Robbinsdale and spent nine more years in the classroom. In 1979 he started the outreach that has become Family Hope Services. He has been married to Dorothy since 1963. They have two grown children and six grandchildren.

Chapter Eleven

TREEHOUSE OUTREACH: OFFERING HOPE TO TROUBLED TEENS

Fred Peterson and Family Hope Services

"Man is born broken. He lives by mending.
The grace of God is glue."

Eugene O'Neil[1]

Having spent his adult life with teenagers, Fred Peterson has had lots of time to study the future in the faces of his restless students. The view has not been encouraging. "It's well known that we are losing our teens," Peterson says. "All you have to do is think of Columbine. Or, you can look at how quickly kids leave the church once they reach high school. They don't leave because they have all the answers about life, but because often their real issues are not being addressed."

Fred's concern for kids goes all the way back to when he took a job as director of an inner-city outreach in Minneapolis after college. The experience of working with these minority teens lit a fire that still burns. Because the teens spent most of their day in school, Fred decided to become a teacher. After getting his credentials he passed up several offers from suburban schools and chose to teach at a residential treatment center for delinquents, the Bar None Ranch for Boys. A year later he and his new wife joined the Peace Corps and spent the next two years training teachers in the West Indies.

When they returned to the States, Fred got his master's degree through a program that placed him in an inner-city Philadelphia school. Once more he worked with socially maladjusted, emotionally disturbed, learning disabled children. Afterward, he settled into the special education program of the Robbinsdale school district near Minneapolis and taught at the junior and senior high levels.

BURNING BUSH

Fred felt deeply the pain and despair of many of his students. Their hopelessness finally drove him to resign from the profession he loved—teaching—in order to address their spiritual and emotional needs more effectively. But people don't just wake up one day and decide to quit something they've been doing for years. The need for a change became obvious to Fred because of what he saw daily in his classroom at Cooper High School. Three incidents in particular combined into a "burning bush" experience for him in 1979.

"The first involved a girl named Stacey," he recounts. "One day she told me her mom had beaten her with a jump rope. She showed me the bruises, plus a set from an earlier beating. She sat down at her desk and hung her head. I said, 'Stacey, you're not very happy, are you?' And she said, 'No, I'm not. I've tried everything. I've tried drugs; I've tried being straight; I've tried running. Mr. Peterson, do you have any other suggestions?' As a Christian I wanted to share my faith, but that's not allowed in the public educational system. So I invited her to come see me after school, but she ran away that day and never returned to the classroom.

"Then there was Bob, another tenth-grader. He broke down a couple weeks later in class, admitting his drug use was out of control. I didn't know what to do, so I sent him to the principal, who put him in detention for drug use. That wasn't the answer.

"The final incident that got me asking what I wanted to be tired from at the end of the day was when Mike shared one Friday afternoon that he was going to a beer bust. I told him to go to a movie, go bowling, call me, do anything else—just don't go to that kegger. He said, 'Don't worry about me, Mr. Peterson.' I didn't think about Mike until next Monday morning when I met the principal at my classroom door. He had come to ask me to be the teacher representative at Mike's funeral. The boy had been run over and killed after the drinking party.

"My students were literally self-destructing before my eyes. These teens all came from broken families; they had no place to take their pain. They were making very poor life-choices because they had lost hope. So I decided I needed to take a step of faith and start working with them in a context where I could also share my faith."

But how would Fred's wife and family respond to his burden? "Dorothy knew I was struggling," Fred says. "She knew I cared more about what was going on in the kids' lives than teaching them reading, writing, and computation. When I told her I'd finally decided to leave my job, I thought she would be nervous about house payments, groceries, retirement money, and caring for our two babies. But through her tears she said, 'I've been praying for two years that you would do this.'"

With Dorothy's blessing and encouragement, Fred resigned to begin a youth outreach in the appropriately named town of New Hope, Minnesota. In time the work was incorporated and the first board chose the name Family Hope Services (FHS) as the work grew and adapted to include ministry to the whole family. The shift was inevitable because, as Peterson quickly learned, "behind every hurting child are hurting parents. I realized we could work with teens all day long, but if we sent them back to abusive, dysfunctional families, we would never work ourselves out of a job. As soon as we caught a vision for 'family hope' instead of 'kid hope,' and changed the original format, things really took off."

To better serve teens and their families, FHS sought licensing as a chemical dependency treatment center and hired qualified staff. Two years later they acquired an even higher level of licensure. The work expanded beyond substance abuse issues to deal with marriage problems, eating disorders, and depression. Basic services were then offered through two divisions: TreeHouse for youth and parents, and Passages Counseling Center for all family members.

SAFE PLACE

The TreeHouse name was suggested by Peterson's daughter Ronda, then in junior high. To her it conjured up the image of a safe place. Today, TreeHouse facilities provide safe places where youth can talk about their problems, find support, learn life skills, and make friends. TreeHouses are also places where adults can receive support and learn parenting skills in a grace-filled environment. School counselors, juvenile courts, probation officers, churches, friends, and families refer teens to TreeHouses.

From small beginnings, FHS has grown to forty-three paid staff (including summer interns) and almost two hundred volunteers. The Christian-based, nonprofit organization now operates five facilities in the suburbs of Minneapolis, with plans to open two more TreeHouses in the next six to eighteen months. They own about three million dollars in assets and positively impact hundreds of lives every year, as Dr. Timothy Geoffrion, executive director of FHS, elucidates:

> We work with over 700 [now 900] youth and hundreds of parents in the course of a year, offering hope and showing them that someone cares. Depression and suicidal tendencies are common. Yet, amazingly, we have lost only one young person to suicide in two decades of ministry. . . .Why? Our model of building caring relationships, combined with providing balanced programs, fosters meaningful life change. Jesus Christ truly makes a life-changing difference in the most difficult of situations, and caring, engaged adults mentor and lead youth to health and wholeness.[2]

Peterson stresses what, to him, is a vital distinction. "The world can get people off drugs, or out of abusive situations, and that's great, but it's not the final chapter. The best the world can offer is rehabilitation, but what people really need is transformation through a new life in Christ."

The presenting problems that bring people to FHS include everything from potential suicides to eating disorders to sexual abuse. From the point of first contact, which is often a crisis situation, the FHS staff works to build long-term relationships with youth and their families. The overall aim of the various programs is to equip people with the skills needed to cope with an increasingly complex and impersonal world. This is done through weekly support groups, activities, trips, retreats, and one-to-one time. Each program is part of a mosaic of caring for the broken and the hurting. Support groups provide opportunities to share struggles or triumphs and to receive and give feedback. Going Deeper groups for youth include teaching on issues like peer pressure, sexual restraint, relationships, and spirituality.

The best the world can offer is rehabilitation, but what people really need is transformation through a new life in Christ.

FHS offers more than talk. After-school and summer activities help kids burn off excess energy in positive ways such as rock climbing, camping, white-water rafting, canoeing, service projects, and weekend retreats. The organization enjoys a broad base of support from both the church and the community-at-large. Their programs are barrier-free and open to all without discrimination. All services, except extended trips, are provided free of charge including transportation, which is provided from door to door.

So who picks up the tab for all this caring?

Much of the funding comes from a committed donor base, but some comes from secular sources. "We receive some funds from local municipalities," Fred explains. "We have been asked by the United Way if we would like their support. They've offered a targeted amount of money for one outreach area and allow us to receive dollars through donor choice. Our model is structured so that government and community dollars go to programs that aren't religious in nature, such as support groups. We are Family Hope Services, but we are also TreeHouse Youth and Parent Outreach. We are very clear that we're faith-based and have a Christian bias. Still, schools invite us in to do support groups and freely refer people to many different TreeHouse activities. We have a twenty-three-year history of being respectful in handling a diverse population while achieving great results."

Guy Rice Doud, National Teacher of the Year for 1986-87, knows about getting results.

> I've seen programs in schools that attempt to work with kids. I've witnessed programs aimed at the parents but I've seen few programs that attempt to encircle the entire family and offer the family an opportunity for healing and the resources needed to get the family "unstuck." Family Hope Services does just what its name implies: it offers hope for today's family. . . .I got very excited when I visited with families who had taken part in the Family Resiliency Project. I said to myself, "This is what families need."[3]

What about those who warn that taking government money will lead to government control? "That has not been our experience," Fred replies. "We are an example of what President Bush is talking about when he stresses the importance of grassroots, spiritually motivated programs that get results. Our approach works well because we develop long-term relationships with kids. We're in full agreement with Dr. Peter Benson of the Search Institute in Minneapolis when he says, 'If we are going to have healthy kids in this society, every kid needs a web of adult connections. Relationships are the oxygen of human development.'

"The Institute has done extensive research on what kids need to hear and learn from those adult relationships," Fred continues. "They've identified forty assets adolescents must acquire in order to increase the odds of staying out of the at-risk category. We've developed a curriculum that addresses nineteen of these assets. Our curriculum doesn't just tell teens what to do; the material actually guides them into making responsible life choices. And what really excites me is that our model and materials are transferable. Others can use our training resources and what we call our Teen-Hope curriculum. In addition, a book that captures the heart of our model, entitled *Getting Kids to Talk*, is to be published soon."

REARVIEW MIRROR

"Looking back on it all now," Peterson says, "I can see how God prepared me and my family for this ministry. My degrees, my teaching skills, the hands-on experiences with troubled kids, my time in the Peace Corps, learning how to negotiate with the public schools—it all came together to help me launch Family Hope Services. On the negative side, sometimes I think I waited too long to make the move. I was thirty-seven years old when I began this work. I would certainly encourage people who are considering a similar change not to delay their decision."

Fred has another caution for would-be social entrepreneurs. "It's foolish to go into the social sector if your spouse doesn't agree 100 percent with the move. After working all day with troubled people, you don't want to come home to a nonsupportive husband or wife. But when there's agreement, there can be great blessing in a lifestyle of service. It's been incredible to see our children develop a heart for God and for wounded people. They saw me leave in the middle of the night because of a suicide call, or watched hurting teens come into our home. It's had a profound impact on who our children have become as adults."

It's foolish to go into the social sector if your spouse doesn't agree 100 percent with the move.

The blessings have been mixed with a few bumps and bruises along the way. "One thing I did poorly at times was hiring," Fred says. "Because we started with a faith-missions model, we took on just about anybody who could raise their own support. At one point we tried to mix this support-raising model with a fee-for-service model and it didn't work. For ten years we had a counseling center with seventeen therapists who were being paid from the fees charged for their services. Putting home missionaries together with those who were getting paid for services created real tension. We have since restructured and from 1993 have referred those who need therapy to other agencies.

"Another thing that hurt us organizationally was my trying to do too much of the work myself. I wore too many hats through the years. I should have brought in expert management help sooner. I have now taken the lead in planning a transition of leadership for the future. This is so critical to the health of an organization, and so difficult to accomplish, especially when the founder is still around. I started the process many years ago and I hope to be part of this ministry for another three to five years. Our new CEO is doing a tremendous job as FHS moves forward."

Peterson advises that planning for leadership succession should begin years in advance—ten years out if possible. "Eighty percent of companies that initiated succession planning ten years or more in advance made the management transition successfully," he cites. "Where succession planning begins between two and ten years before the shift in leadership, the success rate drops to about 50 percent. And when lead time is less than two years, the success rate is only 25 percent."[4]

Planning for leadership succession should begin years in advance—ten years out if possible.

His concern that the ministry he started more than two decades ago outlive his personal involvement reveals that Fred hasn't lost his passion for helping hurting people. "As Christians, we all have the same *Mission*, 'In all we do to bring honor and glory to our God' (see Colossians 3:17), and the same *Commission*, 'Go and make disciples' (see Matthew 28:19-20). While I heartily ascribe to these, it's been my personal *Purpose Statement*, 'To minister the love of Jesus to the least, the last, and the lost,' that's kept me focused. These are the people who still break my heart."

The American family is in need of the triage and emergency care that faith-based groups like Family Hope Services are providing. Certainly there's a personal cost to be paid by spiritual healthcare workers like the Petersons. But if you ask Fred about the pain and problems of his chosen lifestyle, he responds, "There are no such things as problems in ministry, only challenges and opportunities. God has been so faithful. It's absolutely unbelievable the way He has blessed us and given us our hearts' desires to serve Him and help others.

Givers and Receivers
Mark Bjorlo

MARK BJORLO BECAME a "bad actor" when he was in seventh grade at Plymouth Middle School. His parents were getting divorced and he was angry. "I couldn't make sense of the divorce, so I rebelled," Bjorlo said. "That was the beginning of my acting out. But I had a lot of other problems, too. I had a learning disability, and I wasn't a successful student. I was feeling inadequate, I wasn't brainy, and I was pretty small."

Bjorlo is a 1987 Armstrong High School graduate and former TreeHouse youth who got his life back on track and has returned to New Hope (Minnesota) to work with young people. He said he was dealing drugs as an eighth-grader at Plymouth Middle School when he first heard about TreeHouse.

"I was a bad kid—a cigar-smoking, drug-dealing, sailor-talking brat," he said. Bjorlo had been kicked out of confirmation class at the Lutheran church his family attended in Golden Valley after he stole the keys to the building and threw a party in the youth room. He recalls that, about the same time, representatives from the New Hope TreeHouse visited Plymouth Middle School and invited the staff to "pick twelve kids you wish you'd never have to see again."

One of them was Bjorlo.

"That was the first time I'd ever won anything," Bjorlo said. They (the TreeHouse staff) got me with camps and trips. Support groups weren't my cup of tea. But they captured me by inviting me to come and laugh and have fun. I needed to play in a safe way, and TreeHouse was the place for that. There were no hassles."

Soon Bjorlo was coming around for weekly support group meetings and visiting with a staff member one-on-one biweekly. "The staff people at TreeHouse reached out to me in unique and powerful ways by affirming my good actions and not criticizing my bad choices," Bjorlo said. "I got a lot of motivation from the positive affirmation I got at TreeHouse."

But the transformation didn't happen overnight. Bjorlo spent nine months in drug treatment as a ninth-grader, acquiring some skills and tools for dealing with his emotions and life in general. During his junior year in high school, he went to a camp in Colorado with other TreeHouse youths. "Part of that experience made me decide to live my life differently," Bjorlo said. Years later when an area field director job opened in the TreeHouse program, officials contacted Bjorlo and asked if he'd consider coming to work for the program. He returned to New Hope (in 1994) to take the job. "There is a special place in my heart for what goes on here," Bjorlo said.[5]

Today, Mark is a pastor at Grace Fellowship in Brooklyn Park, Minnesota.

FOR MORE INFORMATION, CONTACT
Family Hope Services
3315 Fernbrook Lane North
Plymouth, MN 55447
763-557-8670
www.familyhopeservices.org

BOOKS THAT HAVE INFLUENCED FRED PETERSON
The Power of Alignment: How Great Companies Stay Centered and Accomplish Extraordinary Things, George Labovitz and Victor Rosansky, San Francisco: John Wiley & Sons, 1997.

Flight of the Buffalo: Soaring to Excellence, Learning to Let Employees Lead, James A. Belasco and Ralph C. Stayer, New York: Warner Books, 1994.

Built to Last: Successful Habits of Visionary Companies, James C. Collins and Jerry I. Porras, New York: Harper Business, 1994.

The Divine Conspiracy: Rediscovering Our Hidden Life in God, Dallas Willard, San Francisco: Harper, 1998.

What's So Amazing about Grace? Philip Yancey, Grand Rapids, Mich.: Zondervan, 1997.

The Subtle Power of Spiritual Abuse, David Johnson and Jeff VanVonderen, Minneapolis: Bethany House, 1991.

Dr. Thomas Scott was born in Philadelphia and raised in New York City. He heard the gospel on a troop ship returning from the Pacific at the end of WWII and trusted Jesus Christ. After getting his undergrad degree at Hofstra University, Thom went to Philadelphia College of Osteopathic Medicine. Later he opened a family practice in Delaware City, Delaware. After thirty-three years there, St. Francis Hospital in Wilmington recruited him in 1986 to be the medical director of an HMO, which he ran for five years before starting the St. Clare medical outreach.

Dr. Scott is a member of the American Academy of Family Practice and the Christian Medical Society. He also serves as an elder in his church. Thom and Catherine have been married fifty years. They have two grown children and four grandchildren.

Chapter Twelve

STREET DOCTOR: MOBILE MEDICINE FOR THE HOMELESS

Thomas Scott and the St. Clare Medical Outreach

"Woe to us indeed if we forget the homeless ones who have no vote, no power, nobody to lobby for them, and who might as well have no faces even, the way we try to avoid the troubling sight of them in the streets of our cities where they roam like stray cats."

Frederick Buechner[1]

Being sick is a debilitating experience, but being sick and homeless is disastrous. In a country as affluent as the United States there are upwards of 600,000 men, women, and children who go homeless every night.[2] Officials estimate that families with children comprise 40 percent of this population, while single men make up another 40 percent, single women 14 percent, and unaccompanied minors 4 percent. An average of 22 percent of homeless people in the cities are considered mentally ill; 34 percent are substance abusers; 20 percent are employed; and 11 percent are veterans. The population is estimated to be 50 percent African-American, 35 percent white, 12 percent Hispanic, 2 percent Native American, and 1 percent Asian.[3]

Many Americans are concerned about these displaced masses. A few are doing something to help them, including Dr. Thomas Scott. Inspired by the testimonies of physicians who work with the poor, he has spent time on the streets of Wilmington, Delaware, delivering free healthcare and dignified service to the indigent. Under his leadership, the St. Clare Medical Outreach van gives medical and spiritual care to between twenty-five and thirty patients a day, handling everything from routine immunizations to stab wounds.

The outreach is funded by St. Francis Hospital, several foundations, a local ecumenical group, and private donors. It now serves as the model for mobile units in other cities, including Phoenix, Chicago, Tulsa, Memphis, Baltimore, Camden, and Trenton.

TROUBLED HEART

The impetus behind the St. Clare Medical Outreach comes from the heart of a longtime family physician—a heart that almost stopped beating. Twice! "I survived two heart attacks," says Thom Scott, "and one day I said to my wife, Catherine, 'I belong to the Christian Medical Society, and yet I've never been to one of their national meetings. I'd like to go before I die to see what it's like.' So, we went to Chicago in May of 1991.

"The meeting was entitled 'Share the Vision, Healthcare for the Poor,'" Thom remembers. "It was by far the best medical meeting I've ever attended. The Holy Spirit really motivated and convicted me. At the last session on Sunday, they had a church service. They passed out blue cards for people to make monetary pledges for healthcare to the poor. At the bottom I checked the space marked 'other' and told myself I'd go back to Wilmington and start a work with the homeless. Catherine asked me what I marked and I said, 'I'll tell you later.' I waited until on the plane going home because I knew she couldn't leave me then. She turned out to be very supportive.

"When I got back to Wilmington, Paul King, the CEO of St. Francis Hospital, sat me down and told me they had sold the HMO of which I was the medical director. That meant I no longer had a job. He said he would try to find something for me around the hospital, but I said I wasn't interested. I told him of my pledge to God to start a ministry to the homeless."

At this announcement, Thom expected a pat on the back and a handshake. Instead King explained that the board of trustees had been discussing the fact that the hospital was not really reaching out to people. "One thing led to another," says Thom, "and in time Paul took me to meet Brother Ronald, a Capuchin friar who runs an ecumenical ministry. I asked him for a room somewhere to set up a clinic for the homeless. He said he didn't have an inch of space to spare, which was very disappointing. But then he said, 'Have you ever thought about a mobile clinic?'"

The question got Thom's attention for a very interesting reason. "The night before," he recalls, "I had been reading in a medical magazine and came across a full-page ad about medical vans. For some reason I had torn it out and stuck it in my coat jacket, the very jacket I had on that day. I reached into my pocket, pulled out the ad, and said, 'Do you believe in providence?' Later, Brother Ronald introduced Paul and me to two directors of foundations and they gave us 220,000 dollars to get started."

The Christian Medical Society stayed in touch with Thom after he handed in his commitment card. They called him every few months to see how things were going, always with the caution that, "he not get too excited because it takes two or three years before anybody gets on the road with something like you're trying to do." But in April of 1992, Thom took delivery of his van. "I was out on the streets within eleven months from when I had made my commitment to God. This reinforced to me that it really was His work; I didn't have to worry."

It takes time to learn the nuances and idiosyncrasies of those you want to help, but it's necessary.

While Thom was waiting for his wheels, King sent him to a few places that cared for the homeless. He visited the Pacific Garden Mission in Chicago and Christ Clinic in Washington, D.C. He also went to Boston and Auburn, New York. "The advice they all gave me was always the same," says Thom. "'This is not the ministry to go into if you need immediate gratification.' After years of experience I know what they mean. It takes time to learn the nuances and idiosyncrasies of those you want to help, but it's necessary. Street people, or the chronically poor, have certain traditions and ways they do things. They look upon outsiders with suspicion until they learn they can trust you."

The apostle Paul told believers:

If you help, just help, don't take over; if you teach, stick to your teaching; if you give encouraging guidance, be careful that you don't get bossy; if you're put in charge, don't manipulate; if you're called to give aid to people in distress, keep your eyes open and be quick to respond; if you work with the disadvantaged, don't let yourself get irritated with them or depressed by them. Keep a smile on your face (Romans 12:7-8, MSG).

CARING HOSPITAL

"The key to the mobile unit has been the backing of the hospital," Thom says. "This work wouldn't exist without St. Francis. We operate as a branch of the hospital and come under their licensing. They not only helped me get started, they back the van financially. I raise what I can through foundations and generous individuals like Foster Friess of the Brandywine Fund. I will go anywhere to talk about the van; I don't care where it is. Usually one or two people catch the vision, and the next thing I know, there's a check coming in for fifteen or twenty-five dollars every month. The hospital covers what I don't raise, up to a certain budgeted amount."

In addition to funding, St. Francis does all the X rays and lab work for Dr. Scott's patients at no charge. They hospitalize the homeless when necessary. They are also the base for a network of about ninety physicians and specialists—cardiologists, surgeons, gynecologists— who volunteer their services when needed.

St. Francis is one of two community hospitals in Wilmington. As such, they have clinics for the poor and those who can't afford services. "But a lot of people don't know how to access the clinics," says Thom. "Many of the poor prefer to come to the van because they're seeing the same doctor. Also, it's better to go out to them rather than waiting for them to come to the emergency room. By then it might be too late to do them any good. There's another reason the indigent come to me. It's like a homeless fellow told me the other day, 'You know why we like you, doc?

You're just like us. You're homeless. Other doctors have regular offices, but you just travel around in a truck.' If that's what makes these people bond to me then, thank you, Lord, that's great!"

Beyond financial and professional support, Dr. Scott also receives spiritual encouragement from the nuns at St. Francis. "What we like about you," a sister once told him, "is that you are evangelistic and you're not afraid to speak to people about Jesus Christ." From time to time they call him to come to the hospital and pray with patients who are having difficulties. Being open about his faith and the reasons he's doing this work has never been a problem. He is among the majority of doctors who see the compatibility of faith and medicine.

> A 1996 survey of members of the American Academy of Family Physicians reports that a remarkable 99 percent think religious faith helps patients respond to treatment. The study, conducted by Yankelovich Partners, found that most of these doctors thought spiritual techniques should be part of formal medical training, and 55 percent report they use these techniques as part of their current practice. In fact, the spirituality-health connection is finding a place in medical education. The National Institute for HealthCare Research reports in 1997 that nearly one-third of American medical schools offered courses on spirituality and healing.[4]

Do people try to take advantage of the free medical care? "Of course," says Thom with a grin. "Someone once asked Mother Teresa about being exploited and her reply was, 'How much better to be taken advantage of by the poor than the rich.' What a great answer. For those who abuse the system, we catch them eventually and tell them in a nice way that they don't belong here. This is for people who have nothing."

MOVING VAN
The medical van operates like a bookmobile. "We're out Monday, Tuesday, Thursday, and Friday," Thom says. "Wednesday is for

special projects and van upkeep and repairs when needed. We go to the different dining rooms and shelters where the homeless congregate. The people know our schedule. They have their own means of networking and communicating. From time to time we'll get a lab test back and need to get in touch with a person. Of course they have no address or phone, so we just tell a few of the guys that come in that we're looking for Joe Jones. Two or three days later, Joe shows up.

"Everyone who comes on board is treated as a human being created in God's image. I practice what I call holistic medicine. Since people have a body, a mind, and a soul, you are shortchanging them if you don't deal with all three. So, sharing the gospel and praying with people is part of our routine care. I remember the time a certain lady came back twice and, on her second visit, said, 'There's nothing wrong. I just want you to pray with me.' That overwhelmed and humbled me. The gospel is my life; it's the way I live."

Since people have a body, a mind, and a soul, you are shortchanging them if you don't deal with all three.

Thom's concern for people doesn't end when they leave the van. He often brings homeless men to church with him and has them over for dinner. "I've taken them to the baseball games and picnics to let them know that they're important. They're just as good as anyone else because God created them. He loves them and wants them to find life in Him."

Based on the biblical view of humankind, Phillip Needham of The Salvation Army says,

[I]t is impossible for social service to be perceived as charitable acts toward less fortunate people. Rather, it is to be understood as concrete steps toward realizing the new reality of social reconciliation which has come in Christ. Social service takes place within the new human family which Christ makes possible. There is no condescension in it. It is based upon the deepest respect for persons as potential members of the household of faith.[5]

On Wednesdays, their "day off," the van crew often does special projects like giving physicals to inner-city kids headed to a camp run by the Delaware Association of Chiefs of Police. Then there's the Boy Scout troop in a very poor section of town that also needs physicals. The list goes on. The homeless and inner-city kids aren't the only visitors to Dr. Scott's moving van. Cities like Chicago and Baltimore have shown an interest in mobile, medical outreach. "People who get vans and want to do what we're doing usually come to ride with us," Thom says. "They want to see how we operate. I also get requests to go to other cities, but I don't often accept because I'm too busy here. I want my patients to know I'm committed to them. We're not like some government programs that have started and then fizzled out. That's a difference with faith-based programs such as ours. The people involved are not doing it because it's their job. They're doing it because it's their calling. They have a fire in their bellies, which is one reason they get much better results than most government efforts."

The medical unit that prowls the streets of Wilmington is manufactured by the Moex company. It is the size of an interstate moving van: thirty-five feet long, twelve-and-a-half feet high, and eight feet wide. Thom's office is in the back. Between him and the cab are a multipurpose room and two examining and treatment rooms. The van staff consists of Dr. Scott, Mary Ann Fagan, R.N., who has been with Scott since his Delaware City days, and driver Jim Sculley. A bilingual medical assistant completes the crew since 30 percent of their patients speak only Spanish.

As with the rig in Wilmington, most of the vans in other cities are connected to hospitals that underwrite them. A few are freestanding clinics that raise their own funds. The medical and legal liabilities are just as great as for any doctor, and are usually covered by the hospital's professional liability umbrella. As to their business structure, each medical outreach is set up as an independent nonprofit organization.

Operating costs of the St. Clare Medical Outreach run about

300,000 dollars annually. The figure would be closer to a million dollars if the van crew got paid market value and if services such as X rays, lab tests, and hospitalizations weren't being donated by St. Francis. But even with the hospital's help, there is still plenty of room for old-fashioned, down-on-your-knees faith. "At one time our backs were to the wall financially," Thom reminisces. "We needed medicines for people, but we didn't have any money. Catherine and I were praying about it. One day I got a letter from a lady who lived over a hundred miles away. She said, 'Please use the enclosed check for whatever you want, like buying medicine for patients.' The check was for 4,000 dollars and was a great lesson in faith for me."

It's been said that success without a successor is failure. If you don't pass on your passion, it will die with you. Thom Scott is making sure the work with the homeless and indigent will outlive him by recruiting third- and fourth-year medical and nursing students to help in the van. "I'm seventy-six years old and I'm slowing down," he admits. "I have two other doctors with me now, Eileen Schmitt and Kasimu Moody, who are carrying more and more of the load. The only regret I have about this outreach is that I didn't start it sooner. It's been so gratifying. I've never had so much fun. But I've also never worked so hard. There is great joy in obeying the command to, 'Carry each other's burdens and in this way fulfill the law of Christ' (see Galatians 6:2)."

> *Success without a successor is failure. If you don't pass on your passion, it will die with you.*

"The greatest disease in the West today is not TB or leprosy," said Mother Teresa, "it is being unwanted, unloved, and uncared for. We can cure physical diseases with medicine, but the only cure for loneliness, despair, and hopelessness is love."[6] Dr. Scott and others like him give more than medical aid to the poor. They share God's love the same way the Great Physician did two thousand years ago—by taking it to the streets.

Givers and Receivers

Bernie Thompson, patient

I AM DIABETIC and was sick and needed help. I had been laid off for some time when, one Thursday afternoon in 1992, a nice, clean blue and white van attracted my attention. I stopped and asked several of the waiting people what was happening. They told me the van was there to give free medical care to the homeless and poor. At first I was skeptical and thought this was another community rip-off. But I took a number and waited to be seen.

When I entered the van, I was greeted by Maryann, a nurse who treated me politely, as a person rather than a dog. Next, she introduced me to Dr. Scott, whose kind and caring manner made me feel very comfortable. This was a new experience for me— being treated with respect, warmth, and compassion. Not only did Dr. Scott care for me medically that day, but he also asked about my spiritual life and prayed with me.

The St. Clare van has been a blessing to me both medically and spiritually since that time. I have been a patient there for ten years. I have always felt the love of Christ in the care of Dr. Scott. In fact, he has had me to church with him and to his home for dinner.

Amy Renee Griffin, volunteer

IT'S UNUSUAL to find something that fulfills everything you're looking for and everything you never expected. That happened to me in the summer of my tenth-grade year. I had the amazing opportunity to volunteer with Dr. Thomas Scott on the St. Clare Medical Outreach van. The people who came onto the van had nothing. I saw men and women going through drug and alcohol rehab, and my eyes were opened to a world that I had never seen before.

One of our stops was at Emmanuel Dining Hall West, which attracted many single moms. The children affected me the most and I was able to connect with them in a special way. I remember reading on the floor with two little girls while they waited with their parents for Dr. Scott. I remember comforting a little boy while his stitches were taken out. But the best part of being on the van was watching Dr. Scott. It was easy to see why so many people flocked to the van. He practiced God's love more than medicine, and that was so visible in the responses of the patients and their families. They felt comfortable on the van. They could go there when they needed help because they knew that unconditional love waited for them.

Dr. Scott showed me the same Christian love and attention he showed his patients. He gave me the opportunity to do the preliminary work on several patients, such as measuring temperature and pulse. He also took the time to show me what doctors look for when checking a patient's ears, nose, mouth, and eyes.

It has been my desire to become a doctor ever since I was in fifth grade. The encounter I had with Dr. Scott and the St. Clare medical van gave me insight into the medical field, plus the unexpected blessing of seeing what the true medicine of love can do.

FOR MORE INFORMATION, CONTACT
St. Clare Medical Outreach
c/o St. Francis Hospital
Box 2500
Wilmington, DE 19805
302-575-8218

BOOKS THAT HAVE INFLUENCED THOM SCOTT
Ministries of Mercy: The Call of the Jericho Road, Timothy J. Keller, Phillipsburg, N.J.: P&R Publishing, 1997.

Fearfully and Wonderfully Made, Paul W. Brand and Philip Yancey, Grand Rapids, Mich.: Zondervan, 1997.

City of God, City of Satan: A Biblical Theology of the Urban City, Robert Linthicum, Grand Rapids, Mich.: Zondervan, 1991.

Mourning Into Dancing, Walter Wangerin, Jr., Grand Rapids, Mich.: Zondervan, 1996.

Wake Up America!: Answering God's Radical Call While Living in the Real World, Tony Campolo, New York: HarperCollins, 1991.

Bill Gibbons graduated from Central Washington University, where he later returned to earn a master's degree in reading. As a teacher, he developed a reading program that grew into a business, called HOSTS Learning, which he founded in 1977 and of which he is currently chairman of the board. HOSTS has won numerous awards, including the Blue Chip Enterprise Award from the U.S. Chamber of Commerce as one of the top four small entrepreneurial businesses in America, and the Secretary of Education's Excellence in Compensatory Education Award.

A man in perpetual motion—he has logged over a million miles on three different airlines—Bill crisscrosses the country with the message that underachieving kids like he once was can make something of themselves with the help of caring adults. Bill and his wife, Beverly, live in Vancouver, Washington. They have three children and four grandchildren.

Chapter Thirteen

STUDENT AID: A MILLION MENTORS MAKE THEIR MARK

Bill Gibbons and HOSTS
(Help One Student To Succeed)

"It's not what happens to you; it's how you handle what happens to you that's going to make the difference in your life....It's not where you start—it's where you finish that counts."

Zig Ziglar[1]

HOSTS Learning is the nation's largest, oldest, and most effective academic mentoring program. The program grew out of a Vancouver, Washington, reading lab conducted by a popular teacher named Bill Gibbons. From there it has expanded to impact more than a million children through the efforts of more than a million volunteer mentors. It has won numerous awards and has become a national model for the U.S. Department of Education.

Not a small accomplishment for a man who didn't master the alphabet until he was nineteen.

SLOW LEARNER

The life of Bill Gibbons would have been entirely different if not for the intervention of a caring adult. The help that high school teacher Dick Dibble gave him has been multiplied a million times over through the organization Bill founded. "I always struggled in school," he says with an intensity not dulled by the years. "I can remember being the smartest kid in the dumb class. I enjoyed that because I didn't have to work. That pretty much describes my whole educational experience. Then in my sophomore year I flunked three courses and became ineligible to play football. I decided to drop out. After all, my dad only had a ninth-grade education. I'd be just like him."

Gibbons wasn't dumb; he just did not connect classroom education to real-world success. He was also stubborn enough to refuse to learn something as simple as the alphabet just because a teacher told him he had to. He would have been out the door on the wrong side of a high school diploma if not for the intervention of Mr. Dibble, a world history teacher and debate coach. "He turned my life around," Bill says. "He was the first person, other than my coaches, to say the 'P' word to me. He said I had 'potential' and promised to help me develop it, so I decided to stay in school. He was the hardest teacher I've had at any level. He spent time with me; he encouraged me; he supported me. He is the reason I went on to college and a career in education."

Bill graduated from Central Washington University and took a teaching job in Yakima, Washington. "I started teaching at Adams Elementary School in 1966, one of the lowest performing schools in the city. Eighty percent of my sixth-graders were minority students reading below a second-grade level."

Bill loved the challenge of helping his students, and in his third year in Yakima he was voted Outstanding Young Educator of the Year. In time, he moved from elementary to junior high, where he continued his focus on reading. "If these kids couldn't read, they were doomed to fail. I went back to school and got a master's in reading. I decided I would build a strategy that identified specific learning problems and create a plan that addressed them. I would equip mentors with a customized plan for each student and train the teacher to manage the plan."

The program Gibbons developed became so successful that it was featured in a special broadcast on The Education Channel. He started getting calls from around the country about his ideas. He also received a job offer from Vancouver, Washington, that was too good to pass up. Moving there in 1971 to teach in the Vancouver School District, Gibbons created HOSTS as a reading-room program that grew to serve three hundred children. "The acronym stands for Help One Student To Succeed," Bill explains. "It comes from Psalm 103:21, 'Bless the Lord all you His hosts, you servants of His, doing His will.'"

As had happened in Yakima, Gibbons was voted Outstanding Young Educator of the Year in Vancouver, this time at the high school level. He had written a book and was touring the country, speaking on educational issues. But his life had a hole in it. "I was not a Christian at this point," he says. "My success was actually destroying me. I wasn't happy. But my wife had a peace and I asked her about it. I knew she loved the Lord, and as she shared with me about her faith, in time she led me to Christ. I was thirty-two years old."

"After I accepted the Lord," Gibbons continues, "I felt the need to step out of public education and to create HOSTS as a ministry. I kept praying, 'Lord, if you want me to do this, show me how.' And the answer came back to start a nonprofit business instead. So in 1977, after eleven years in public education, I left to start a non-profit, research-based organization. The M. J. Murdock Charitable Trust funded my efforts for the first few years. I was able to carry out my research and perfect the concept of structured mentoring based on Dr. Benjamin Bloom's research on mastery learning published in *The Two Sigma Effect*."

*S*ocial entrepreneurs have to determine if a nonprofit or for-profit structure is best for the long-term viability of their vision.

Gibbons began putting the program into the Vancouver schools. Other schools also started implementing it. However, he wasn't set up to handle the expansion and it became apparent that the nonprofit structure wouldn't work. The question of structure is an important one. Social entrepreneurs have to determine if a nonprofit or for-profit structure is best for the long-term viability of their vision. The wrong framework will severely restrict growth, as Bill soon discovered. When he went back to the Murdock Trust and applied for a million dollars, they told him they wouldn't keep supplying the kind of resources HOSTS needed. Instead, they offered to help him create a for-profit company, which he did in 1984.

The decision appeared to be a disastrous one as Gibbons proceeded to lose a million dollars over the next two years. "I had never run a business before," he confesses. "I didn't know anything about cash flow. Those were the hardest two years of my life. I lost all my family's resources. After the second Christmas with no presents under the tree, I told Bev, 'I have bankrupted our family. I'm going to quit.' She looked at me and said, "No, you're not. God didn't say it would be easy. He told you to do this, and you will do it.'"

As he thinks back, Bill candidly admits, "I was arrogant and proud. God had to do some work on my personality. He didn't change my aggressiveness, but the first lesson I had to learn was humility. God used those two years to humble me and show me that I couldn't do anything without Him."

STUMBLING FORWARD

Gibbons followed the example of comedian Jonathan Winters, who once said, "I couldn't wait for success, so I went ahead without it." His fledgling company went through some pretty dark times. "At one point I couldn't make payroll," Bill recounts. "It got to where some employees came to me and said, 'Bill, we can't work here anymore. We've got to feed our families and we're just not making it.' I said, 'I understand. For those of you who stay, I will give you shares in the company. I know they're not worth anything now, but someday they will be. And those who need to go can go.' One person left and five people stayed."

Experiences like these convinced Bill that he needed help, which the Lord soon provided in the form of qualified people. "I've been greatly blessed by some key team members who joined the company when it was very small and who have taken on responsibilities that I didn't have the ability to handle. Sheila Tretter, our COO, has done a terrific job in directing product development and managing our customer support personnel across the nation. Another key person has been CFO Dan Hunt, who has helped me understand that we have to have a sound financial structure if we're to continue working with children in the future. Robert Schaefer, former Washington state Speaker of the House, has been my personal mentor. He is a wise teacher who helps me see how Christ is using even the difficult experiences to shape my life.

"While I may not have understood the basic principles of business at first," Bill goes on, "as a Christian I did know about operating by faith. I refused to sue two clients who had not paid their bills, which totaled over a million dollars. In time they both made good on their debts. I was able to pay my staff their back wages, plus 10 percent interest."

By their third year, HOSTS broke even. Over the next several years they became profitable. "When we reached nearly a hundred employees," says Gibbons, "it became apparent that I needed to keep filling key positions with professionals who had a level of expertise we lacked on the inside. Since we spent every extra dime on research, I didn't know how to get the cash to hire these people. Enter Joe Ritchie, a man who had owned CRT, the largest options trading firm in America. Joe had once written a check to have a HOSTS program implemented in a school near him. After he sold CRT, he came to me with a proposal. In essence he said, 'I have made a lot of money and want to invest in something that will give back to society. I believe HOSTS is the vehicle to do that.'"

Joe became the principal shareholder of the company, and the infusion of cash allowed HOSTS to hire additional expertise. "Joe is a very humble man," says Bill. "God has used him in a mighty way in my life and in our company. In the last five years we have grown from doing seven million dollars in business annually to nearly twenty million. To date we have served over a million children through over a million mentors. We are now in over thirty-eight states, El Salvador, and Puerto Rico. We have become one of the premier education programs in the country and have received the Outstanding Educational Contribution Award from the Department of Education and the Secretary of Education's Excellence in

Compensatory Education Award. Also, the Department of Justice has designated us as a national model for promoting safe schools and reducing teen pregnancies, school violence, and the use of drugs and alcohol. Most recently, HOSTS was identified as a national model in the conference report attached to President Bush's *No Child Left Behind Act* of 2001."

This significant success has been built on a solid foundation comprised of the company's four mission statements. "The first is honoring God in all that we do," Bill explains. "This means acting with integrity. There must be consistency among our beliefs, actions, and goals. We must live what we believe and serve our employees and customers with ethical behavior. The second statement says we will enthusiastically do the right things the right way. We will do the right things because they are right and for no other reasons. Doing things the right way means making excellence a habit, not an exception.

> *There is no mission for an organization without a profit margin, but profit margin must never drive the mission.*

"The third value we have is to help make people successful. We strive to create environments where people can experience the joy of success. Since all people are made in the image of the Creator, they are creative. They can use that creativity to grow into the person God intends them to become. We want to be the kind of place where that can happen. And the fourth statement says we will invest our talents for maximum return. There is no mission for an organization without a profit margin, but profit margin must never drive the mission. We strive to grow profitably in both our experiences and our finances, believing that God honors those who honor Him with pure motives."

SUPERIOR RESULTS

On this principled foundation, HOSTS has developed a very effective educational product. They provide a structured plan that links trained community volunteers, business partners, and mentors with students needing extra help. Lesson portfolios are individualized according to the students' personal needs and are consistent with their learning styles, skill levels, and interests. The program is appropriate for students in any learning environment because they are allowed to progress at their own pace.

Instruction is designed and monitored by the HOSTS teacher and delivered by a trained volunteer mentor. The mentor follows lesson plans created by HOSTS specialists with the use of a comprehensive electronic database. "We have to improve our schools in a way that makes sense economically," Bill insists. "This is where mentoring comes in. We give people a way to give back to a system that is essential to our country's future."

HOSTS also helps teachers, principals, and superintendents meet their educational objectives. Moreover, a HOSTS school or district can administer its programs without increasing staff or adding to teacher workload. Outside the classroom, "Partnership with Parents" workshops help involve parents in their child's academic activities. Parents are encouraged to become HOSTS mentors for other children. This is one way the program recruits the more than 100,000 mentors involved annually in its programs.

HOSTS not only works with parents, but has formed strong relationships with leading businesses such as Kellogg, The Limited, Inc., General Motors, Hewlett-Packard, Steelcase, Inc., USA Today, and Wal-Mart. "HOSTS is about supplying real-world structured solutions to schools to get students back on grade level," says Kathy Devine, USA Today Education, national projects manager.

Les Wexner, CEO and chairman of The Limited, Inc., says, "The Limited provides over eight hundred employees to mentor in the Columbus Public Schools' HOSTS program. We chose HOSTS as our vehicle for school improvement because it is structured and accountable, provides excellent staff, and gets results." Indeed, in a federal multi-state impact study, HOSTS student gains exceeded the national average by 50 percent. That's why the Education Commission of the States (ECS) has designated HOSTS as a proven mentoring program and put them on their "Best Practices" list.

Involving parents and businesses in the educational process is not the extent of Bill Gibbons' vision for HOSTS. Since becoming a Christian he has continually sought to integrate his faith with his work. One expression of this has been the company's efforts to recruit mentors for public schools from within churches. Local churches are great places to find the hearts and hands needed to build a brighter future.

"We've been able to help churches get involved in community development," Bill says. "For instance, there is a Nazarene church in southeast Los Angeles that has a recreational program for kids. They have a facility where kids can play basketball almost all night. The upstairs is set aside for academics, and they have selected HOSTS for their reading and math programs. They teach the kids to read and do math and give them a place to spend their time in productive recreation. The program has been so popular that the public schools are contracting with the church for their services."

> *Local churches are great places to find the hearts and hands needed to build a brighter future.*

Bill cites another example from the other side of the country. "We are working with a ministry in Raleigh, North Carolina, called Neighbor to Neighbor. They went into the downtown area and started a church in an abandoned warehouse, and are using HOSTS to help kids academically." These kinds of partnerships are particularly exciting to Bill because of his original desire to start HOSTS as a ministry. "God said 'no' to that," Bill reflects, "but what He did was take us in the direction of serving in public schools. And now churches and other ministries are using what we developed to help kids. It's very exciting!"

Bill Gibbons counts himself a fortunate man because he's been able to spend the majority of his time and resources focused on one purpose—changing lives. Through HOSTS, he is helping millions of young people and adults reach their full potential.

Mr. Dibble would be proud of his star pupil.

Givers and Receivers
Marsha Smitly

TAKING ON THE ROLE of HOSTS Coordinator was way out of my league, coming from a medical background and being a stay-at-home mom for thirteen years. But being involved with HOSTS has turned my world upside down.

One of our pastors, Royce Hathcock, approached me in 1998 and asked me to pray about coordinating a literacy program our Neighbor to Neighbor Ministries wanted to begin. After praying for three days, God gave me scriptural confirmation from Isaiah 58-60 that He was calling me to this ministry.

Bill Gibbons came to Raleigh to share about HOSTS a few weeks later. When I heard him speak, I not only felt confirmed that this was what I should do, but I felt totally inadequate for the job! I spoke with Bill and he assured me I had all the qualifications needed to do this: GOD had called me and HE would do the equipping. I asked God to call another woman who felt the same passion and He answered my prayer in calling Alison Kerr as my assistant. So the journey began.

Although the enormous task of beginning this ministry was daunting, God continually brought to mind the Scripture He had given me. In Isaiah 60, He challenged us to "arise and shine." We were to be a light in the darkness and to trust Him to bring the resources we needed for this dream. His promise from verse 10 was that foreigners—people we did not know—would rebuild our walls. And that's exactly what has happened.

The building we have is an old warehouse offered to us free of charge by a man we didn't even know. We have renovated a small area to run the HOSTS program. God has brought many people and organizations across our path who have provided money, building materials, labor, furniture. . .the list goes on. HOSTS has been a wonderful catalyst to bring people together from all walks of life. Our desire is not only to help children academically, but to offer them hope and spiritual healing as well.

It's exciting to see how God is drawing youth from the neighborhood. I think of one young man whose involvement in HOSTS as a student drew his sister to come and hang out at the warehouse. She became a mentor and now their mother is involved. This year she is going to mentor as well.

What a unique privilege I have to see confidence rise in the students as their reading improves and as they experience an adult's genuine care for them. We are seeing lives changed and new hope born in both youths and adults who are opening their lives to one another. The need is great and we at Neighbor to Neighbor are small, but God is expanding HOSTS in our area through other organizations that have seen the success of our program. It is true—there's no limit to what God can do through anyone totally committed to Him.

FOR MORE INFORMATION, CONTACT
HOSTS Learning
8000 N.E. Parkway Drive, Suite 201
Vancouver, WA 98662
800-833-4678
www.hosts.com

BOOKS THAT HAVE INFLUENCED BILL GIBBONS
Jesus CEO: Using Ancient Wisdom for Visionary Leadership, Laurie Beth Jones, New York: Hyperion, 1996.

The Heart of an Executive: Lessons on Leadership from the Life of King David, Richard D. Phillips, New York: Doubleday, 1999.

Fix Schools First: Blueprint for Achieving Learning Standards, Jack E. Bowsher, New York: Aspen Publishers, 2001.

Making Schools Better: How Parents and Teachers Across the Country Are Taking Action—And How You Can Too, Larry Martz, New York: Random House, 1995.

Seizing the Future: The Dawn of the Macroindustrial Era, Michael G. Zey, New York: Transaction Publishing, 1998.

Daniel Dominguez was born in Buenos Aires, Argentina. After graduating from high school, he moved with his family to Houston, Texas, where he received a B.A. in 1968 and a master's of accountancy in 1970 from the University of Houston. That same year he became a U.S. citizen and received his CPA license. He became a partner at BDO Seidman, LLP in 1977. He is a member of the International Tax Forum and the International Fiscal Association.

Daniel has served on the boards of several charitable and civic organizations, including the Texas Youth Camps, the United Way Allocations Committee, and the Star of Hope, Houston's largest organization working with the homeless. For many years he has also been an elder at Spanish Bible Fellowship. He married Noemi while a junior in college. They have four grown children and live in Houston.

Chapter Fourteen

PREVENTATIVE
MAINTENANCE

Daniel Dominguez and the
Christian Family Center

"The people who have done extraordinary work on behalf of their organization, their community, their country, or their society have spoken of the knowledge that they were being used by forces higher than themselves. That is what drove them to take that important first step towards personal responsibility."

Joseph Jaworski[1]

To many Anglos in the southern U.S., Hispanics are just laborers from the northern part of Mexico, people who do the tasks others don't want to," says Daniel Dominguez, International Tax partner at BDO Seidman, the world's sixth largest accounting firm. "But we represent the fastest growing population segment in the country, increasing four times faster than the population as a whole. Immigration also adds to our numbers. The Immigration and Naturalization Service estimates that for each immigrant who becomes a citizen there are at least four blood relatives who will also become U.S. residents."

The Annie E. Casey Foundation reports that 36 percent of the greater Houston population under the age of eighteen is Hispanic. In 1998 Hispanics accounted for 51 percent of all births in the city.[2] "However, while our numbers are expanding," Dominguez says, "our core family values are rapidly deteriorating. Hispanic youth lead in the dubious categories of dropout rate, crime, and gang activity in Houston according to the Texas Education Agency.

There's a definite correlation between lack of education and being in a correctional institution. Eighty-five percent of prison inmates are high school dropouts and the percentage of Hispanics in jail is much higher than among the general population."

SOBERING STATISTICS

These statistics are painful to Daniel, who has a heart for the Hispanic population of his adopted hometown. After moving to Houston from Buenos Aires, he worked his way through college as a busboy and parking lot attendant. After graduating with his CPA, he joined Seidman and Seidman, which later became BDO Seidman, LLP. Today the accounting and consulting giant has over 22,000 personnel worldwide, revenues of over 2.4 billion dollars, and a presence in almost one hundred countries.

"Being in international business is very exciting," Daniel says. "There's always something to learn, someplace to go, someone to meet. But my passion is for my fellow Hispanics who haven't had the same opportunities I have. The economic realities of our population in general, and of immigrants in particular, often require both parents to work outside the home. The resulting lack of supervision allows young people to drift into delinquency. Lack of education and language skills further feed the negative cycle. Many of our youth have become disenfranchised by the lack of family support and structure. Why do they join the gangs? They need to know who they are. They long to be part of something bigger than themselves. Unless we restore our culture and provide successful role models, these kids will be lost."

Daniel cites a study conducted by the Carnegie Foundation showing that many adolescents spend up to 40 percent of their day without adult supervision. According to law enforcement officials, the peak hours of violent crimes committed by youth are from 3 p.m. to 6 p.m. weekdays. The National Campaign to Prevent Teen Pregnancy reported in May of 1999 that Latinas had the highest teen birth rate of any ethnic group in the U.S., accounting for approximately one quarter of teen births in 1997.

This concern for his people has led Dominguez and the

congregation of Spanish Bible Fellowship (*Verdad en Amor*), where he serves as an elder, to take action. In order to reverse the negative trends, they decided to do some preventative maintenance *before* the fact and not wait until after Hispanics became statistics. In 1994, they created the Christian Family Center (CFC) with a mission to restore the home, unite families, and bring them closer to God.

This was a big undertaking for the small, nondenominational church. "Adult attendance at that time ranged between 100 and 120," Daniel recalls. "After we sold our small building to develop the CFC, we spent three years renting space at a Bible college. At one point our numbers dropped to 130. But since we moved into the Center's new building, total attendance has gone up to 380 and 450 per Sunday.

"It is sometimes embarrassing when I show the drawings for the Center site and ask people to invest. Many laugh when they find out the size of our church. Yes, the project is impossible for a small church, but it's not impossible for a big God."

Daniel often asks prospective investors if they know the story about the man walking on the beach and throwing starfish back into the sea? When asked how his puny efforts could possibly make a difference, the man picks one up, throws it back, and replies, "It will make a difference to that one." Daniel then explains, "CFC isn't trying to change the world; we simply want to make a difference where we live. Building more jails or passing out more condoms won't fix the problems facing our kids. We have to touch their lives one at a time."

This grassroots community activism is the best, most realistic hope for a better future. The idea is sometimes heard in minority rhetoric that it's the government's responsibility to fix social ills. But this is a false hope, as no less a thinker than Peter Drucker observes:

> We increasingly realize that modern government is not capable of taking care of community and social problems. Nor is the free market. There is a growing awareness of the

need for a new sector. . . .In this sector, citizenship as a working "volunteer" once again becomes a reality rather than a ritual consisting of voting once in a while and paying taxes.[3]

SMALL CHURCH, BIG VISION

Here's how Spanish Bible Fellowship is making a difference. The church created a separate social service organization that bought a fifteen-acre site to house its programs. These programs serve the needs of the community as a whole, but focus primarily on Hispanics. The present campus includes a multi-purpose building with ten classrooms, an auditorium, a soccer field, basketball and volleyball courts, and a swimming pool.

Several programs are already operating in the partially completed facilities, including English as a Second Language classes, parenting classes, youth and adult leadership training, family counseling, soccer clinics, summer day camps, swimming lessons, and senior citizens' events. Then there's the Team Kid Program for lower-income Hispanic youth in self-care between 3 P.M. and 6 P.M. As facilities are completed—especially the gymnasium—additional programs and services will be added, such as AA and ACOA (Adult Children of Alcoholics) meetings, crisis pregnancy counseling, computer literacy classes, and midnight basketball. Even though the Center is still under construction, several hundred people go through its programs every week.

Meeting physical needs will only produce short-lived results unless people also experience a spiritual change.

Dominguez concurs with the other social entrepreneurs in this book when he says, "You have to meet people's felt needs first. If those are physical, they have to be addressed. But meeting physical needs will only produce short-lived results unless people also experience a spiritual change. The spiritual aspect of what we're doing is the key. We start with the surface problems, but work toward the root issues, which are spiritual. I remember what Dr. Tony Evans once said regarding the extraordinary transformation that corn kernels experience under heat to become popcorn—the change comes from within."

The Center isn't a Bible school; however, the values it teaches and models are drawn from Scripture. "We believe it's good that kids play basketball instead of rob stores," says Daniel. "But just keeping them busy on Friday nights isn't going to prevent them from stealing at other times. Our goal is to see them changed from the inside out through the gospel of Jesus Christ.

"It would be easier for the Center to be totally separate from the church for fund-raising reasons," Dominguez says, "yet that was never a consideration. Part of what we want to do is to involve and motivate our own church kids. Most have had a fairly comfortable life and just doing the 'church thing' isn't enough to challenge them to live for God. They are a big part of making this whole thing work. They are the future. However, a person doesn't have to be a Christian to benefit from, or work with, the CFC. We have no qualms with pre-Christians getting involved. There are a lot of people who have a social conscience and who want to help. We have volunteers that don't go to church and we get the chance to share Christ with them."

For his part, Daniel has done everything from operating a backhoe to teaching leadership classes at the Center, but his main role has been in donor relations. His efforts so far have raised over a million and a half dollars for CFC. Most of the money has come through contacts Daniel has developed in his more than thirty-five years of working in and around Houston.

Proverbs 22:1 says, "A good name is more desirable than great riches; to be esteemed is better than silver or gold." Daniel agrees. "A good reputation is better than just about anything else. You have to work hard to earn it, especially when you live in the same town for over three decades and you keep running into the same people. It makes a big difference when going for a grant if somebody knows you or your reputation."

The impact of Daniel's credibility begins in his own firm. "BDO Seidman committed twenty-five thousand dollars to the Center if I would personally match their gift," Dominguez reveals. "Other companies followed suit, committing five or ten or twenty thousand dollars, many times on a matching basis. This kind of arrangement is win-win because what's good for the community is good for business.

"At Seidman we believe the more our people are involved in social causes and civic organizations, the better known our firm becomes and the more business we will generate. BDO has encouraged me to be active in the social sector because they realize if people believe in me as a community member, they are more likely to trust me with their financial affairs. Individuals of different faiths have invested in CFC, including Jews, Muslims, and Hindus. They may not understand, or have an interest in, the spiritual side of the Center, but because of personal trust, they know their money will be well spent. A Jewish foundation gave us one of our first grants—115,000 dollars—even though they were white and we were brown, they were Jews and we were Christians—as the foundation manager pointed out."

Many nonprofit ventures don't get funded, or else are financial disasters, because they don't address the business side of what they're trying to do.

Not only does Daniel lend his reputation to CFC, but he brings his considerable business acumen to bear on its behalf. "Many nonprofit ventures don't get funded, or else are financial disasters, because they don't address the business side of what they're trying to do," he points out. "To prevent this, skilled business people are needed to bring a level of sophistication to social organizations in ways that will encourage investors. A businessperson's ability to analyze, organize, and put the dream onto a spreadsheet can make the vision viable to others. For example, when I present our business plan to potential donors, I include an operations budget. Without an operations budget in place, you won't reach shrewd investors who don't want their gifts to be in vain, which would be true if there are no funds to operate once construction is complete."

While nonprofits should be able to demonstrate their financial viability, they are different from for-profit businesses, as Drucker noted in a 1996 interview with *Inc.*

Inc.: But so many people in business are leery of non-profits because they see them as nonprofessional.

Drucker: And they're both right and wrong. They're right because far too many nonprofits are either poorly managed or not managed at all. But they're wrong because nonprofits are not businesses and should be run differently.

Inc.: In what way?

Drucker: They need more, not less, management, precisely because they don't have a financial bottom line. Both their mission and their "product" have to be clearly defined and continually assessed. And most have to learn how to attract and hold volunteers whose satisfaction is measured in responsibility and accomplishment, not wages.[4]

SUCCESS REDEFINED

Daniel has experience in both settings and knows that success is defined differently in each. However, he has his own personal definition. "I define success as being satisfied with life. This comes about through finding and fulfilling one's calling. For me, this means working hard to structure international transactions for my firm's clients. But it also means working hard to build a family, a church, and a community."

Of course the danger of an ambidextrous lifestyle is having too much "to do" left at the end of the week. "I struggle with the time pressures," Daniel acknowledges. "I get frustrated when things fall through the cracks before I can get to them. I'm so thankful that my family has been involved in the church and the Center, but I know they've paid a price for my busyness. Based on my own experience I would say to other social entrepreneurs, don't sacrifice life's important things for results that may come about anyway, even with less time devoted to them."

> *Don't sacrifice life's important things for results that may come about anyway, even with less time devoted to them.*

In his powerful little book *Tuesdays with Morrie*, Mitch Albom tells of his visits with his favorite college professor, Morrie Schwartz, who is suffering from Lou Gehrig's disease. With the clarity of the dying, Morrie tells his friend:

"Remember what I said about finding a meaningful life?. . . Devote yourself to loving others, devote yourself to your community around you, and devote yourself to creating something that gives you purpose and meaning. . . ."

He paused, then looked at me. "I'm dying, right?"

Yes.

"Why do you think it's so important for me to hear other people's problems? Don't I have enough pain and suffering of my own?

"Of course I do. But giving to other people is what makes me feel alive. Not my car or my house. Not what I look like in the mirror. When I give my time, when I can make someone smile after they were feeling sad, it's as close to healthy as I ever feel.

"Do the kinds of things that come from the heart. When you do, you won't be dissatisfied, you won't be envious, you won't be longing for somebody else's things. On the contrary, you'll be overwhelmed with what comes back."[5]

"One of the best parts of my life," Daniel agrees, "is being able to touch and help others, to give back a little of what I've been blessed with. When I'm at the Center on weekends or early in the mornings, I can almost see the soccer games going on. I can almost hear the kids at the swimming pool. I listen in my heart to the noise of hundreds of people buzzing in and out. I watch my own children being active here, leading other young adults in helping our neighbors. That's my dream! I'm not interested in seeing my name on any of the buildings. If I'm remembered at all, I want it to be as someone who pointed others to Jesus Christ. I can't think of a better legacy."

Givers and Receivers
Bill Boras

WHEN I WAS YOUNG my mother was killed in an airplane accident that I myself barely survived. The loss deeply affected my father, who became emotionally and physically abusive. A few years later, one of my brothers died and another descended into alcoholism and drug addiction. I bore the brunt of my father's anger over these family tragedies.

Daniel Dominguez has been a friend of my father since they were young. I've known Daniel all my life. He talked to me at church and made an effort to connect with me even when I became very rebellious. I had become a Christian at eight years old and I attended the youth group. But as I got older, I chose not to live the Christian life and went my own way.

At one point, my father and I had a big fight and we stopped talking. I ran away from him because I feared what might have happened if we fought. My lifestyle got more and more destructive. I was dating a topless dancer and getting drunk every day. I remember calling Daniel one night when I was terrified I might die. He talked to me for about an hour and calmed me down.

Everything came to a head for me on a snow-skiing trip with friends. I was so depressed I stayed in the lodge and contemplated suicide. I cried out to God and told Him if my life didn't change

I didn't want to live anymore. When I got home I went to the Christian Family Center and talked to Daniel. I appreciated that he had established a relationship with me when I was a kid and had never ever stopped loving and paying attention to me. He helped me get my life turned in the right direction and was very influential in my breaking free from drugs and alcohol and the fast lifestyle.

Today I am one of the leaders of the youth group based at CFC. I graduated from the University of Arizona with a degree in psychology and work with abused kids and a juvenile probation program. I spend much of my spare time at the Center. My goal in life is to follow Daniel's example of helping people, whether on the job or off. From him I've learned that love never stops. It's a lifestyle.

FOR MORE INFORMATION, CONTACT
Christian Family Center
P.O. Box 1828
Sugar Land, TX 77487
713-986-3139
www.centrofamiliarcristiano.org

BOOKS THAT HAVE INFLUENCED DANIEL DOMINGUEZ

Halftime: Changing Your Game Plan from Success to Significance, Bob Buford, Grand Rapids, Mich.: Zondervan, 1994.

The Ascent of a Leader, Bill Thrall, Bruce McNicol, Ken McElrath, San Francisco: Jossey-Bass, 1999.

Who Moved My Cheese?: An Amazing Way to Deal with Change in Your Work and in Your Life, Spencer Johnson, Kenneth H. Blanchard, New York: Putman, 1998.

The One Minute Manager, Kenneth Blanchard, Spencer Johnson, New York: Berkley Books, 1983.

Agape Leadership, Robert L Peterson, Alexander Strauch, Littleton, Colo.: Lewis & Roth, 1991.

Biblical Eldership, Alexander Strauch, Littleton, Colo.: Lewis & Roth, 1986.

Tom Mason is one of three executive vice presidents at Focus on the Family. After a long career with General Motors, he took early retirement in 1997 and moved to Colorado Springs to join Focus. He has a bachelor of mechanical engineering from the GM Institute and an M.B.A. from Michigan State University. During his thirty-six-year tenure with GM, he held senior management positions in New York, Salt Lake City, Atlanta, and Detroit. In 1988 he became vice president of sales, services, and parts for GM Europe, and in 1992 he was named vice president of marketing for their Canadian operations.

He and his high school sweetheart, Karen, have been married since 1963. They have four grown children and five grandchildren.

Chapter Fifteen

KEEPING AMERICA FAMILY-FRIENDLY

Tom Mason and Focus on the Family

"There are few matters of more profound public consequence than the condition of marriage and families. Most of our social pathologies—crime, imprisonment rates, welfare, educational underachievement, alcohol and drug abuse, suicide, depression, sexually transmitted diseases—are manifestations, direct and indirect, of the crack-up of the modern American family."

William J. Bennett[1]

Just how much trouble is the American family in? Former Secretary of Education William Bennett offers the following sobering summary in his book *The Index of Leading Cultural Indicators 2001*:

> During the 1990s, the out-of-wedlock birth ratio increased 18 percent, the percentage of families headed by a single parent increased 13 percent, the marriage rate decreased 9 percent, and the number of cohabiting couples increased 48 percent. It is important to place these developments within a historical context. They follow three decades of dramatic, and deeply harmful, changes in the American family. According to the distinguished historian Lawrence Stone, "The scale of marital breakdown in the West since 1960 has no historical precedent." The family is the fundamental unit of society, and cultural, demographic, economic, and political factors have weakened the bonds that used to hold us together. I believe that the break-up of the American family is the most profound, consequential, and

negative social trend of our time.[2]

No one has done more to stop the erosion of the traditional family than Dr. James Dobson, founder of Focus on the Family. "Nothing short of a great Civil War of Values rages today throughout North America," he insists. "Two sides with vastly differing and incompatible worldviews are locked in a bitter conflict that permeates every level of society."

Starting with a weekly radio program in 1977 that aired on a few dozen stations, Focus has grown into an international organization with scores of ministries and over 1,300 employees. Its daily broadcasts are heard on about 6,000 facilities worldwide. Its ten magazines are sent to more than 2.3 million people monthly. The ministry responds to as many as 55,000 letters a week—it has its own zip code—and offers professional counseling and referrals to a network of 1,500 therapists. Focus also addresses public policy and cultural issues.

Helping Dr. Dobson carry the weight of one of the largest Christian ministries in the country are three executive vice presidents. One of them is a guy who used to sell cars.

FIRST HALF

Tom Mason grew up in an agnostic home. His wife, Karen, was raised in a church home but didn't have a personal relationship with Christ. "We were both twenty years old when we got married," says Tom, "and for our first ten years together we phased in and out of a mainline denomination. Our children came along and there were times when we dropped them off at Sunday school and went for coffee. All that changed when GM moved us to Birmingham, Alabama, in 1974. Over the next year both Karen and I independently found the Lord."

Shortly after the Masons became believers, they got tuned in to Christian radio and heard Dr. Dobson. "We had small children then," Tom recalls, "and over the years the Focus broadcasts really ministered to us. On a trip to Switzerland one year we met Mike Yorkey, who at that time edited *Focus* magazine. We struck up a friendship that became an annual Christmas card relationship.

"Around Christmas in 1996, I awakened to the fact that I'd been with GM almost thirty-six years. Since I started at age eighteen, I could take early retirement with full benefits although I was only fifty-three. That year, when Mike called for the holidays, I told him what I was thinking."

"Funny you should mention that," Mike replied. "We're looking to fill some key positions at Focus. Can I throw your name into the discussions?"

Tom was open to whatever the Lord wanted. "I had a deep respect for this ministry but I never thought about working at Focus. Over the next several months I exchanged calls and letters with Focus. Karen and I visited Colorado Springs and met with Dr. Dobson and others. Then in April of 1997, I accepted the position as one of three executive vice presidents and started my new job in June.

"When I weighed the prospects of taking early retirement and doing something in Christian work, I wrestled with self-doubt. But two things helped me move ahead. First, a godly friend gave me Bob Buford's book *Halftime*. Buford had passed through—and written about—all the evaluations and thought processes I was going through. His words reassured me. The other thing was that the Lord worked through a hundred different circumstances to confirm His direction. Time and time again He validated that this was what I was supposed to do. In fact, He validated it so many times I finally concluded He must think I'm as dumb as a post; that's why He had to keep repeating Himself."

There is a deep and abiding pleasure in doing something that has cultural relevance and eternal significance.

With refreshing candor, Tom adds, "Another insight that helped me as I struggled with this decision was something Karen told me. 'You know, Tom, you don't have to do this. But if you don't, someone else will get the blessing.' I've been at Focus for five years now. When I think of the people I've gotten to know, the experiences I've had, and the contribution I've been able to make, there's no question my life would have been so much less had I missed coming here. There is a deep and abiding pleasure in doing something that has cultural relevance and eternal significance."

New challenges

While there has been a learning curve for Mason at Focus, it hasn't been too steep. "I'm constantly amazed at how relevant almost everything I did in corporate life is to what I do today. The executive VPs here are in charge of the administrative part of this ministry, including the budgeting process. A great deal of what I did in corporate life actually prepared me for what I'm doing now. GM had more zeros in their budget, and the emphasis on profit and product was different, but the accounting and business principles are the same."

After Tom had been at Focus a few months, Dr. Dobson asked him what surprised him the most in coming from GM to Focus. "I told him I was astonished by the hostility of the culture to the things of God. In secular life, my exposure to this hostility was limited as I would see bits and pieces on a broadcast or read something in the paper. But being here in a senior position, I'm overwhelmed by the animosity toward the things of God. To stand for biblical truth in this culture is to invite incredible hostility." Former Solicitor General and Supreme Court nominee Robert Bork explains part of this antagonism.

We can hardly ignore the government when, by constitutional right, we comprise the government. . . .Now all of us who love our faith and also our nation must decide how best to express that care.

> Liberals of the modern variety are hostile to religious conservatism in any denomination. They realize, quite correctly, that it is a threat to their agenda. For that reason, they regularly refer to the "religious right" using the term

as a pejorative to suggest that anything conservative is extreme. No conservative, religious or secular, ought to accept the phrase. Modern liberals try to frighten Americans by saying that religious conservatives "want to impose their morality on others." That is palpable foolishness. All participants in politics want to "impose" on others as much of their morality as possible, and no group is more insistent on that than liberals. Religious conservatives are not authoritarian. To the degree they have their way, it will be through democratic processes.[3]

"How can Christians dispense grace in a society that seems to be veering away from God?" asks Philip Yancey, who goes on to partially answer his own question.

> The Bible offers many different models of response. Elijah hid out in caves and made lightning raids on Ahab's pagan regime; his contemporary Obadiah worked within the system, running Ahab's palace while sheltering God's true prophets on the side. Esther and Daniel were employed by heathen empires; Jonah called down judgment on another. Jesus submitted to the judgment of a Roman governor; Paul appealed his case all the way to Caesar.

> To complicate matters, the Bible gives no direct advice for citizens of a democracy. Paul and Peter urged their readers to submit to authorities and honor the king, but in a democracy we the citizens are the "king." We can hardly ignore the government when, by constitutional right, we comprise the government. . . .Now all of us who love our faith and also our nation must decide how best to express that care.[4]

The people at Focus have chosen to express their love for God and this nation by "disseminating the gospel of Jesus Christ to as many people as possible, and, specifically, to accomplish that objective by helping to preserve traditional values and the institution of the family." They do this in a comprehensive way. Their communication efforts generate a constant stream of radio and television programs, magazines, books, films, and videos. Their Personal Touch Ministries include a chaplaincy program, a CEO Forum, a crisis pregnancy program, an Institute for select college students, and a General Benevolent Fund that distributes over 1.5 million dollars annually.[5]

"We are committed to excellence in ministry," Mason emphasizes. "What we do in God's name should always be done well. This applies to institutions as well as individuals. I've noticed that some ministries tend to be strong on faith and conviction but weak on organization and business skills. There's no excuse for this. Colossians 3:23 tells us to do all things as unto the Lord. This includes everything from administration to how funds are raised to how people are treated.

"Dr. Dobson is absolutely committed to this. That's why we respond to each and every constituent who calls or writes in a way that matches emotion for emotion. We call this *E for E*. It also means being good stewards. We believe the resources the Lord brings us are to be used in His service. Every dollar is what we call *blood money* on the part of our donors. We don't have any condos in Hawaii. We don't have any airplanes. Dr. Dobson doesn't take a salary. We don't stockpile any funds or budget for a surplus. We plan next year's budget based upon the level of resources the Lord has brought us this year. He has been faithful over the years to honor this Manna Principle."

Nonprofits must periodically evaluate their efforts and discontinue programs that aren't doing what they're supposed to— good stewardship requires it.

Tom believes that "the bottom line at Focus—or any church or parachurch organization for that matter—is ministry. We have about eighty different ministries under the Focus umbrella. Some of them are benevolent; they don't pay for themselves. They cost far more than any revenue they produce. But there is no hesitancy in underwriting these programs if they are a good ministry value.

"A for-profit corporation is obviously in a different situation," he clarifies. "For example, a company may produce a product that has a large following, but when the economics become such they can't make money with that product, it's their responsibility to stop producing it. Their ultimate accountability is to their shareholders. Ministries are different, but they aren't above scrutiny. Nonprofits must periodically evaluate their efforts and discontinue programs that aren't doing what they're supposed to—good stewardship requires it."

PERSONAL ADVICE

For those approaching, or living through, the midlife years, Tom has some personal advice. "I would encourage people reaching their forties to spend time with God seeking His will for their futures. They should read some of the great material that's been written by those who have made successful transitions, like Bob Buford. His metaphor of life as a 'game' is very helpful. At some point, they should get alone in the locker room and ask, 'I played the first half with this focus; how am I going to play the second half?' Some will conclude they don't want to change a thing. That's fine. They still need to ask the question, though."

Here is how Buford describes the scenario:

> In the first half of life, there is barely enough time to go beyond second base. We are hunter-gatherers, doing our best to provide for our families, to advance our careers, and to pass our beliefs and values on to our children. In addition, for most men, and certainly a growing number of women, the first half finds us in our warrior mode. We need to prove to ourselves and others that we can accomplish something big, and the best way to do that is to become increasingly focused and intense. I think of the first half as a season in which to develop faith and learn more about the unique way the Bible approaches life. The second half, when the pressure lets up, seems to be more the time when most people round second base and begin to do something about the faith they've developed.[6]

Mason also offers a word of caution. "I have had young men with young families tell me of their desire to go to the mission field. That may be exactly the right thing for them to do, but I remind them that their most important mission field is their family. To do something that will benefit others, but at the same time be harmful for your family, is a bad trade. Anything you do, no matter your motivation, is probably not the right thing if it hurts your spouse or children."

Based on 20/20 hindsight, are there things Tom would do differently? "Certainly!" he exclaims. "You sometimes hear people say later in life, 'I wouldn't have done anything differently.' Well, baloney. The Lord has blessed me greatly. I have a wonderful wife and a great marriage. We have four great children and five precious grandchildren. I wouldn't change any of that. But I've made mistakes along the way that I regret. I've lost my temper on occasion, and I can honestly say that not once when I've lost my temper has the outcome been good. I would like to go back and take another run at trying to develop a relationship with my parents that I never really had. Also, I would worry less, because as I look back, there is no question that the Lord had me in His hand every step of the way."

To do something that will benefit others, but at the same time be harmful for your family, is a bad trade.

With his trademark ambiguity, baseball great Yogi Berra once said, "When you come to a fork in the road, take it." To which baseball fan Tom Mason would add this encouragement: "It's one thing to come to a road you've often thought about going down— say to a ministry or a more spiritually significant job – and quite another thing to actually take it. For me, I'd been with GM for two-thirds of my life. I was comfortable and competent. I could have stayed there for another twelve or thirteen years. Switching directions was challenging and intimidating, but it's also been a great opportunity to trust God in new ways.

"I have a plaque in my office that reads, 'What we are is God's gift to us. What we become is our gift to God.' I want to make the most of my life for Him. There have been challenges along the way, but I wouldn't turn back from the joy I've found for anything in this world."

Givers and Receivers
Excerpts from letters

MY CAREER PATH has included a couple of high-level positions with *Rolling Stone* magazine and MTV. I stumbled upon the Focus website during an Internet search, and because of my background I was naturally drawn to the Plugged-In page. I was absolutely bowled over by the intelligent, open-minded, discerning reviews of the various recordings. Your evaluators obviously listen carefully and take the time to think deeply about their reviews; that is something that most critics, Christian and secular, fail to do even on the most basic level. Having recently embarked on a serious lifestyle change, I applaud your mission even as I continue to struggle with my own personal issues. Keep up the good work!

SEVERAL YEARS AGO, after a lengthy period dealing with financial difficulties and the stress of parenting three children, I descended into severe depression. We sought help from our pastor and church leaders, but none of their well-meaning suggestions brought any relief. Finally my husband called Focus on the Family. We were counseled over the phone by one of your wonderful staff experts. He referred us to a Christian counselor near our home and sent us some very insightful resources. That was the beginning of my re-entry into life. I have no doubt that I would have eventually been hospitalized, were it not for your ministry showing us the first few steps out of the pit. We now have four great kids and a sound marriage—life is good. THANK YOU!

ABOUT A YEAR AND A HALF AGO, I was facing some difficulty in my marriage and needed advice, but could not afford a counselor. My sister suggested I contact Focus on the Family. I called after-hours, but your receptionist took my name and information. A counselor returned my call the next day. In a brief session, probably less than half an hour, he listened intently and then helped me face up to my situation. He was sympathetic, but he was also frank about issues I needed to address in my own heart. That short conversation helped me get back on track, and since then my marriage has greatly improved. I have recommended your services to friends and family.

DEAR ODYSSEY:

My name is Abigail and I am ten years old. I am writing because of the Adventure you played today. I had really long hair, but we found out last March that I have diabetes. I took shots for a few weeks, and then my hair started getting thin and scraggly. I decided to cut ten inches off my hair and give it to "Locks of Love" (they make wigs for kids who lose their hair to cancer). My mom cut my hair this morning. I was having a really hard time about having short hair. Then it was time to listen to Odyssey, and you played a story about Karen, a girl who had cancer in her leg. Listening to the story made me know that some kids have it worse than me and I had cut my hair for a good reason. It makes having short hair more bearable because it seems like God is smiling at me.

FOR MORE INFORMATION, CONTACT
Focus on the Family
Colorado Springs, CO 80995
800-232-6459
www.fotf.org

BOOKS THAT HAVE INFLUENCED TOM MASON

Halftime: Changing Your Game Plan from Success to Significance, Bob Buford, Grand Rapids, Mich.: Zondervan, 1994.

Margin, Richard A. Swenson, Colorado Springs: NavPress, 1992.

The Soul Winner: How to Lead Sinners to the Savior, Charles Haddon Spurgeon, Grand Rapids, Mich.: Eedrmans, 1994.

The Death of Outrage: Bill Clinton and the Assault on American Ideals, William J. Bennett, New York: Touchstone Books, 1999.

The Screwtape Letters, C. S. Lewis, Nashville: Thomas Nelson, 1993.

My Years with General Motors, Alfred P. Sloan, New York: Doubleday, 1996.

A Final Word

Six Action Steps
to Get Personally Involved

We began this book with six rules of engagement for social entrepreneurs and we'll close it with six action steps for those who want to progress beyond reading to doing. If the stories in between have inspired you, here's what you can do about it.

STEP ONE: *GET YOUR FEET WET.*

Pick two or three chapters that stirred you the most and check out the websites of those organizations. If you like what you find, contact them for more information. See if you can get involved as a volunteer. If they don't operate in your community, is there a local organization that does similar work? Or, can you explore the possibility of bringing the organization to your city, school, or church?

"The most effective SEs don't just quit their day jobs and jump into the abyss," says Bob Buford. "They test their way in, often by running low-cost probes to find out the nature of this new environment called 'church' or 'hospital' or 'community organization.' They adopt a beginner's mindset and start small."

Gary Larson drew a *Far Side* cartoon that shows a caveman tied on top of a large stone wheel perched on the crest of a hill. Another caveman waits below, clipboard in hand. The caption reads, "Early experiments in transportation." We learn best by doing, so don't be afraid to experiment.

STEP TWO: *EXPAND YOUR VISION.*

Follow your heart into ministry, but don't forget your mind. Review the recommended reading sections in each chapter and make a list of six to ten books to read over the next year. Choose titles that will inform and equip you for ministries that interest you. Conduct a bit of informal research. Follow the advice of Juan Benitez and find out which people and organizations "have a good return on investment (ROI) in the form of changed lives." Study those whose clients are being transformed, whose programs are cost effective and efficient, and whose business practices reflect integrity and a strong sense of stewardship.

Learn from the best, and then apply that knowledge to your own investments of time and money.

STEP THREE: *CHART YOUR PROGRESS.*

If you sense the Lord leading you to get more involved in serving others, review Buford's rules of engagement in light of your own situation.

Do you have a sense of what God is doing around you?

Have you taken an honest inventory of your strengths? (Remember, you can't give away what you don't have.)

Have you looked into a parallel career to test the waters?

Do you have a "BHAG," a **B**ig, **H**airy, **A**udacious **G**oal?

Can you pull together a team to help you carry out your vision?

Has your passion been tempered in the fires of adversity and survived?

Put your name in the blank space at the bottom of the chart on page 23. Mark the columns that apply to you. Note what needs work and develop an action plan to address those areas.

STEP FOUR: *SEEK PERMISSION AND ADVICE.*

Any expenditure of time or resources in the social sector should be discussed with your spouse and family. "It's foolish to go into the social sector if your spouse doesn't agree 100 percent with the move," says Fred Peterson. And don't forget Tom Mason's warning: "To do something that will benefit others, but at the same time be harmful for your family, is a bad trade. Anything you do, no matter your motivation, is probably not the right thing if it hurts your spouse or children."

Ask for advice from those who know you best—your family and friends. If the Holy Spirit is opening up an area of service, ask Him to confirm His direction through others.

STEP FIVE: *AVOID A "SAVIOR" COMPLEX.*

Don't bite off more than you can chew. Remember the counsel of Sean Lambert: "When it comes to the daunting task of helping the poor—or anyone for that matter—start small. Those who do too much too soon often get discouraged and quit." Not even Jesus assumed the mantle of "total responsibility," as Philip Yancey points out:

> The syndrome of unhealthy self-sacrifice for the sake of others, of bearing more of a person's pain than the person herself, is sometimes called a "savior complex." Ironically, the true Savior seemed remarkably free of such a complex. He caught a boat to escape crowds; he insisted on privacy and time alone; he accepted a "wasteful" gift of perfume that, as Judas pointed out, could have been sold, with the proceeds used to alleviate human misery. Jesus healed everyone who asked him, but not everyone he met.[1]

Although Jesus did not meet every need He saw, He could still say to His Father at the end of His earthly ministry: "I have brought you glory on earth by completing the work you gave me to do" (John 17:4). Jesus let His calling focus His caring.

We can't do everything, but we can do something. So how do we discern what that "something" is? The answer is found in one of Jesus' most famous parables.

STEP SIX: *BE A GOOD SAMARITAN.*

The term "social entrepreneur" is just a modern synonym for "Good Samaritan." The phrase comes from a story Jesus told to a cantankerous lawyer who wanted to know the extent of his social responsibility.

A man was going down from Jerusalem to Jericho, when he fell into the hands of robbers. They stripped him of his clothes, beat him and went away, leaving him half dead. A priest happened to be going down the same road, and when he saw the man, he passed by on the other side. So too, a Levite, when he came to the place and saw him, passed by on the other side. But a Samaritan, as he traveled, came where the man was; and when he saw him, he took pity on him. He went to him and bandaged his wounds, pouring on oil and wine. Then he put the man on his own donkey, took him to an inn and took care of him. The next day he took out two silver coins and gave them to the innkeeper. "Look after him," he said, "and when I return, I will reimburse you for any extra expense you may have."

Which of these three do you think was a neighbor to the man who fell into the hands of robbers?

The expert in the law replied, "The one who had mercy on him."

Jesus told him, "Go and do likewise" (Luke 10:30-37).

The Good Samaritan responded to a need that he encountered in his everyday life (as have the people featured in this book). He wasn't moved by a report about the dangerous traveling conditions on the Jericho Road but by the sight of a bruised and bleeding man. The man's condition moved the Samaritan to compassion, "a deep awareness of the suffering of another coupled with the wish to relieve it." The Samaritan could have done what the priest and Levite did, come up with an excuse why he couldn't get involved. Instead, he took the time to help the destitute stranger. He gave his money to someone who needed it more. He saw to the victim's future well-being by making provisions to cover ongoing expenses.

"Go and do likewise," Jesus told His listeners.

What needs have we personally encountered?

What moves us to compassion?

What resources has God given us to share?

What is the Holy Spirit prompting us to do?

Most of us won't be called to start national organizations or minister to the multitudes, but Jesus makes it clear all of us are called to be good neighbors. That's where love starts.

Only God knows where it might lead.

Contact Information

Best Friends Foundation
4455 Connecticut Avenue, N.W.
Suite 310
Washington, DC 20008
202-237-8156
www.bestfriendsfoundation.org

Bethesda Associates/Mission of Mercy
15475 Gleneagle Drive
Colorado Springs, CO 80921
719-481-0100
www.missionofmercy.org

The Center for *Faith*Walk Leadership
125 State Place
Escondido, CA 92029
800-728-6000
www.faithwalkleadership.com

Christian Family Center
P.O. Box 1828
Sugar Land, TX 77487
713-986-3139
www.centrofamiliarcristiano.org

Circle Urban Ministries/Rock of Our Salvation Church
118 North Central Avenue
Chicago, IL 60644
773-921-1446
www.circleurban.org

Colorado Christian University
180 S. Garrison Street
Lakewood, CO 80226
303-963-3399
www.ccu.edu

Enterprise Development International
10395 Democracy Lane
Fairfax, VA 22030
800-936-2253
www.endpoverty.org

Family Hope Services
3315 Fernbrook Lane North
Plymouth, MN 55447
763-557-8670
www.familyhopeservices.org

Focus on the Family
Colorado Springs, CO 80995
800-232-6459
www.fotf.org

Friends of the Children
44 N.E. Morris
Portland, OR 97212
503-281-6633
www.friendsofthechildren.com

Homes of Hope
100 West 35th Street, Suite C
National City, CA 91950
619-420-1900
www.ywamsandiegobaja.org

HOSTS Learning
8000 N.E. Parkway Drive, Suite 201
Vancouver, WA 98662
800-833-4678
www.hosts.com

InnerChange Freedom Initiative
Prison Fellowship Ministries
1856 Old Reston Avenue
Reston, VA 22180
703-478-0100
www.prisonfellowship.org

Leadership Network, or, HalfTime
2501 Cedar Springs, Suite 200
Dallas, TX 75201
214-979-2431 (Leadership Network)
www.leadnet.org
214-720-0878 (HalfTime)
www.halftime.org

Neighborhood Ministries
1918 W. Van Buren Street
Phoenix, AZ 85009
602-252-5225
www.neighborhoodministries.org

St. Clare Medical Outreach
c/o St. Francis Hospital
Box 2500
Wilmington, DE 19805
302-575-8218

Notes

Preface

1. Peter Drucker, quoted by George Gendron, "Flashes of Genius," *Inc.*, May 15, 1996.
2. Jack Kornfield, quoted by Anne Lamott, *Bird by Bird* (New York: Pantheon Books, 1994), p. 205.

Introduction

1. Heather R. McLeod, "Crossover," *Inc.*, May 15, 1997.
2. Henry T. Blackaby and Claude V. King, *Experiencing God: How to Live the Full Adventure of Knowing and Doing the Will of God* (Nashville: Broadman & Holman, 1997), p. 129.
3. Peter Drucker, quoted by George Gendron, "Flashes of Genius," *Inc.*, May 15, 1996.
4. Mark Henricks, "In the BHAG," *Entrepreneur*, August, 1999.
5. Zig Ziglar, *Over the Top* (Nashville: Thomas Nelson, 1997), p. 246.
6. Bob Buford (*Halftime: Changing Your Game Plan from Success to Significance*, Grand Rapids, Mich.: Zondervan, 1994), p. 167.
7. Richard C. Levy, *The Inventor's Desktop Companion* (Canton, Mich.: Visible Ink Press, 1995), p. 4.

Chapter One

1. Garry Wills, *Certain Trumpets: The Call of Leaders* (New York: Simon & Schuster, 1994), p. 270.
2. Stephen Caldwell, "Gung-ho for God," *Life@Work*, November/December 1999.
3. Ken Blanchard, *We Are the Beloved: A Spiritual Journey*, self-published, 1994, p. 43.
4. Eugene Peterson, *The Message: The New Testament in Contemporary Language* (Colorado Springs: NavPress, 1993), p. 368.
5. Blanchard, pp. 86-87.
6. Gregg Levoy, *Callings: Finding and Following an Authentic Life* (New York: Harmony Books, 1997), p. 31.

Chapter Two

1. Galatians 2:10, New International Version.
2. John Ortberg, *If You Want to Walk on Water, You've Got to Get Out of the Boat* (Grand Rapids, Mich.: Zondervan, 2001), p. 60.
3. Robert A. Watson and Ben Brown, *The Most Effective Organization in the U.S.: Leadership Secrets of The Salvation Army* (New York: Crown Business, 2001), pp. 92-93.

4. Heather R. McLeod, "Crossover," *Inc.* May 15, 1997.

5. McLeod.

Chapter Three

1. Martin Luther King, Jr., quoted by Philip Yancey in *Soul Survivor: How My Faith Survived the Church* (New York: Doubleday), p. 29.

2. Raleigh Washington and Glen Kehrein, *Breaking Down Walls: A Model of Reconciliation in an Age of Racial Strife* (Chicago: Moody Press, 1993), pp. 107-108.

3. Washington and Kehrein, p. 241.

4. Eleanor Josaitis, "Personal Histories," *Harvard Business Review*, December, 2001, p. 32.

5. Josaitis, p. 32.

Chapter Four

1. Cal Thomas, "Sex Industry Seeking Customers," *The Washington Times*, June 10, 2001.

2. www.bestfriendsfoundation.org/about.html.

3. Mona Charen, "These Teens Know How to Say No," *Reader's Digest*, March 1997.

4. The Today Show, 6/7/01.

5. Sarah Brown, Director of the National Campaign to Prevent Teen Pregnancy.

Chapter Five

1. Bob Metcalfe, founder of 3Com, quoted by Scott Kirsner, "Nonprofit Motive," *Wired*, September, 1999, p. 117.

2. *Wonderful Peace*, text, W. D. Cornell, music, W. G. Cooper, *The Hymnal for Worship and Celebration*, Waco, Texas: Word Music.

3. Max Lucado, *The Applause of Heaven* (Dallas: Word Books, 1990), p. 82.

4. Judy Wicks, quoted by Ben Cohen and Jerry Greenfield, *Ben & Jerry's Double Dip: Lead With Your Values And Make Money, Too* (New York: Simon & Schuster, 1997), p. 179.

5. Mark McCormack, *What They Still Don't Teach You at Harvard Business School* (New York: Bantam, 1989), p. 225.

Chapter Six

1. William J. Bennett, *The Broken Hearth: Reversing the Moral Collapse of the American Family* (New York: Doubleday and Colorado Springs: Water-Brook, 2001), p. 93.

2. *Standing at a Crossroads*, InnerChange booklet.

3. William Mattox Jr., "Prison Program Uses Faith to Transform Lives," USA Today, March 15, 1999.

4. John Eldredge, *Wild at Heart: Discovering the Secret of a Man's Soul* (Nashville: Thomas Nelson, 2001), p. 175.

5. Gayle Johnson, "One Man's Turnaround," *The Dallas Morning News*, August 28, 1999. Reprinted with permission from The Dallas Morning News.

Chapter Seven
1. Bob Buford, unpublished interview.
2. Gregg Levoy, *Callings: Finding and Following an Authentic Life* (New York: Harmony Books, 1997), p. 302.
3. Tom Hallman Jr., "The Guide," *The Sunday Oregonian*, July 11, 1999.
4. Hallman Jr.
5. Margery Stein, "For Every Child, a Full-Time Friend," *Parade*, May 28, 2000.
6. Hallman Jr.

Chapter Eight
1. Steve Sjogren, *Servant Warfare* (Ann Arbor, Mich.: Servant Publications, 1996), p. 93.
2. Personal correspondence to Sean Lambert.

Chapter Nine
1. Mother Teresa, *A Simple Path* (New York: Ballantine Books, 1995), pp. 80-81.
2. *2001 KIDS COUNT Data Book*, The Annie E. Casey Foundation, Baltimore. (Statistics use 1998 data.)
3. Mother Teresa, p. 89.
4. David Holmstrom, "A Church Opens Doors For Kids on the Street," *The Christian Science Monitor*, March 4, 1996.
5. Amy Sherman, "100 Things the Church Is Doing Right," *Christianity Today*, November 17, 1997.
6. Merrill Oster and Mike Hamel, *The Entrepreneur's Creed* (Nashville: Broadman & Holman, 2001), p. 159.
7. Howard Schultz, *Pour Your Heart Into It* (New York: Hyperion, 1997), p. 201.

Chapter Ten
1. William Holmes McGuffey, quoted by D. James Kennedy and Jerry Newcombe, *What If the Bible Had Never Been Written?* (Nashville: Thomas Nelson, 1998), p. 20.
2. Scott Adams, *The Dilbert Future* (New York: HarperBusiness, 1997), pp. 86-87.
3. D. James Kennedy and Jerry Newcombe, *What if the Bible Had Never Been Written?*, p. 245.
4. Larry Donnithorne, *The West Point Way of Leadership: From Learning Principled Leadership to Practicing It* (New York: Doubleday/Currency, 1994), p. 97.

Chapter Eleven
1. Eugene O'Neil, quoted by Anne Lamott, *Traveling Mercies: Some Thoughts on Faith* (New York: Pantheon Books, 1999), p. 112.

2. Family Connection newsletter, Spring, 2001.

3. Guy Rice Doud, personal letter to supporters of the Family Resiliency Project, August 31, 1994.

4. Excerpted from a Christian Management Association workshop, "Succession Planning: Preserving the Future by Planning it Now," Russell G. Robinson.

5. Excerpted from Sue Webber's, "'Bad Actor' Sets New Scene," *New Hope-Golden Valley Sun Post*, March 27, 1996.

Chapter Twelve

1. Frederick Buechner, *The Longing for Home* (San Francisco: Harper Collins, 1996), p. 140.

2. U.S. Department of Health and Human Services, http://aspe.os.dhhs.gov/progsys/homeless/.

3. The U.S. Council of Mayors 17th Annual Conference Survey of Hunger and Homelessness, December 17, 2001, www.usmayors.org/uscm/news/press_releases/documents/hunger_release. htm.

4. Richard Cimino and Don Lattin, *Shopping for Faith: American Religion in the New Millennium* (San Francisco: Jossey-Bass, 1998), p. 46.

5. Phillip D. Needham, quoted by Robert A. Watson and Ben Brown in *The Most Effective Organization in the U.S.: Leadership Secrets of The Salvation Army* (New York: Crown Business, 2001), pp. 228-229.

6. Mother Teresa, *A Simple Path* (New York: Ballantine Books, 1995), p. 79.

Chapter Thirteen

1. Zig Ziglar, *Over the Top* (Nashville: Thomas Nelson, 1997), p. 54.

Chapter Fourteen

1. Joseph Jaworski, quoted by James E. Liebig, *Merchants of Vision: People Bringing New Purpose and Values to Business* (San Francisco: Berrett-Koehler, 1994), p. 15.

2. *Child Trends KIDS COUNT Special Report, Houston, Texas*, The Annie E. Casey Foundation, Baltimore.

3. Peter Drucker, quoted by Bob Buford, *Halftime: Changing Your Game Plan from Success to Significance* (Grand Rapids, Mich.: Zondervan, 1994), p. 14.

4. George Gendron, "Flashes of Genius," *Inc.*, May 15, 1996.

5. Mitch Albom, *Tuesdays with Morrie* (New York: Doubleday, 1997), pp. 127-128.

Chapter Fifteen

1. William J. Bennett, *The Broken Hearth: Reversing the Moral Collapse of the American Family* (New York: Doubleday and Colorado Springs: Water-Brook, 2001), p. 4.

2. William J. Bennett, *The Index of Leading Cultural Indicators 2001*, Washington D.C.: EMPOWER.org., 2001, Executive Summary, p. 2.
3. Robert H. Bork, *Slouching Toward Gomorrah: Modern Liberalism and American Decline* (New York: HarperCollins, 1996), p. 337.
4. Philip Yancey, *What's So Amazing about Grace?* (Grand Rapids, Mich.: Zondervan, 1997), p. 241.
5. www.family.org/welcome.
6. Bob Buford, *Halftime: Changing Your Game Plan from Success to Significance* (Grand Rapids, Mich.: Zondervan, 1994), p. 29.

A Final Word
1. Philip Yancey, *Church: Why Bother?* (Grand Rapids, Mich.: Zondervan, 1998), p. 88.